D1434683

A JOURNEY THROUGH INTELLECTUAL PROPERTY RIGHTS

DESIGNING
YOUR OWN
UNIQUE AND
DAZZLING
LIFE

Ho Hyun Nahm

Patent Attorney

You can also become a Creative Minority
that can move human civilization.

Your life will be filled with joy when you
shine "your own unique, dazzling light."

A Journey Through
Intellectual Property Rights

authorHOUSE®

by Ho Hyun Nahm

- **QUALIFICATIONS - PROFESSIONAL EXPERIENCE IN INTELLECTUAL PROPERTY**

  Ho-Hyun Nahm is an internationally respected and recognized patent attorney and leading authority in the practice of international intellectua l property law. Born in Youngdong Choongbuk Province, Korea in 1953, he obtained his LL.B. from College of Law at Choungju University in 1976 and M.P.A. from the Graduate School of Public Administration at Seoul National University in 1985. He served as a Partner at Central International Law Firm from 1987 to 1996. He founded his firm, H.H. Nahm International Patent & Law Firm, in September 1996. As of July in 2006, he established a strategic co-alliance partnership with Barun law-a major firm in Korea and changed the name of firm to BARUN IP & LAW.

- **ACTIVITIES - KOREA AND INTERNATIONAL**

  - Advisory Member, Presidential Advisory Council on Science & Technology, a Constitutional institution serving as an advisory board to the President of the Republic of Korea (2005-2006)
  - President, Korea Chapter, Asia Patent Attorneys Association (APAA) (2012-2015)
  - President, Korea Trademark Society (1999-2000)

- Chairman, Korean Internet Address Dispute Resolution Committee (2014 - 2016), Chairman of APAA Trademark Committee (2003-2009); Current Coordinator of National Group Presidents' Meeting of APAA (2015 – present); Current Vice President of Intellectual Property Forum under Korean National Congress; Current Panelist on U.S. National Arbitration Forum (NAF), World Intellectual Property Organization (WIPO), Asian Domain Name Dispute Resolution Committee (ADNDRC), Czech Arbitration Court (CAC), Panelist of Korean Internet Address Dispute Resolution Committee (2002 - 2016)
- Current Arbitrator on Hong Kong International Arbitration Centre(HKIAC), Korean Commercial Arbitration Board.
- Member, Korean Industrial Property Law Association, Intellectual Property Forum, International Trademark Association (INTA), European Communities Trademark Association (ECTA), Pharmaceutical Trademarks Group (PTMG), MARQUES, the Association Internationale pour la Protection de la Propriété (AIPPI)
- Director and Member, Korean Chapter of Fédération Internationale Des Conseils En Propriété Intellectuelle (FICPI)
- Director of International Affairs (March 2000-February 2002) and Member, Korean Patent Attorneys Association

■ AWARDS

- Selected as one of "The World's Leading in Trademark Law" in 1996 by 'Euromoney Publications PLC' based in London
- Selected as "Leading Intellectual Property Lawyers in Asia Pacific," "Most Highly Acclaimed Legal Experts in the Intellectual Property Practical Areas(s)," "Highly recommended Asia-Pacific focused Lawyers in the Intellectual Property Area(s)" for 7 straight years (2007-2013), by 'Asia Law'

- Recognized as the 'Man of the Year in Law 2010' by American Biographical Institute (ABI)
- Awarded as the "Winner of the 2010 New Quality Innovation Award (Service Innovation)" for the first time by a professional in the field of patents and legal services in Korea
- Awarded "Award in Writing" from the Korean Academy of Invention Education (2015)

■ BROADCASTING • PUBLISHED ARTICLES • BOOKS

Mr. Nahm hosted a weekly TV show and appeared in broadcasting frequently, spoke at international occasions numerously, wrote a great number of articles and books some of them recorded best seller. For details, please refer to APPENDIX.

Phone: +82-2-3479-7000
E-mail: hh-nahm@barunip.com
Website: www.barunip.com

AuthorHouse™ UK
1663 Liberty Drive
Bloomington, IN 47403 USA
www.authorhouse.co.uk
Phone: 0800.197.4150

Published by AuthorHouse 09/26/2017

ISBN: 978-1-5462-8189-4 (sc)
ISBN: 978-1-5462-8190-0 (hc)
ISBN: 978-1-5462-8212-9 (e)

CONTENTS

PROLOGUE

FIRST EXPERIENCE IS HEART-POUNDING EXHILARATION

Fall of 2016 marked my 30th anniversary of passing the Korean Patent Bar as well as the 20th anniversary of my firm. It has already been 17 years since I published my first book, "Challenging the 21st Century with Intellectual Property Rights," which was once on the bestseller list and also prepared in English and Japanese versions.

If my first book, "Challenging the 21st Century with Intellectual Property Rights," is recounting the stories of the first half of my life as a patent attorney specializing in intellectual property, my new book, "Designing Your Own Unique and Dazzling Life," qualifies as marking the footprints of the second half of my life.

American men, in most cases, love to talk about cars and sports. With Korean men, the conversation will inevitably center around their exploits while serving in the military. Of course, men everywhere also cannot leave out talk about women - probably just as much as women talk about men in their chatters.

History of civilization all evolves around stories. Arnold Joseph Toynbee, a noted historian and cultural critic, once proclaimed that human life and existence have meaning when "creative minorities" rise to the occasion to deal with "challenges" of the time.

I have always looked forward to telling my grandkids, when they get old enough, of the "heroic" exploits of my life. I can tell them how much their grandpa enjoyed his life; how good and wonderful his life has been; and how much their grandpa hopes that they can likewise enjoy their own lives... I wanted to do this while holding their hands, walking in joy. I could whisper these stories to them while outdoors and looking up the sky in the dark of the night.

But it dawned on me that I may already be gone from this world before my grandkids became old enough for me to have an intellectual discussion of this nature with them. I had foolishly forgotten or perhaps tried hard to ignore the fact that God could call me up at any time.

While my grandkids would have a chance to read about a portion of my life through "Challenging the 21st Century with Intellectual Property Rights," I thought that it would be a good idea to complete the sequel and leave it on the record sooner than later. Of course, I would most certainly hope to live long and healthy enough to tell these stories to my grandkids personally.

So I started writing with some urgency. I do not wish to write about someone else's life or stories that others have left behind. I want to convey the story of my own unique and dazzling life as a patent attorney and intellectual property specialist and as a sincere and earnest "creative minority." With humility, I wanted to bear witness to how interesting, fulfilling and wonderfully exciting life can be when you live with the belief of the "power of positive force."

Regardless of the nature of one's work or education, people strive to achieve their "creative best" output. As a result, one can enjoy the sweet memory of dynamic stories of someone saving a person's life or rescuing a family or even a nation.

I can easily imagine how rewarding it would be for a doctor to apply his or her own creative craft to save a person's life despite 1% chance of success. My story does not fall under the same category as saving a life though.

However, it does include stories where I was able to assert my best creative approach to overturn established Supreme Court cases, leading to a new precedent. On many occasions, I enjoyed a great sense of elation over dramatic and even miraculous results of overcoming established norms which were achieved only when I was able to combine "creative mind" with "best efforts."

I have personally experienced how the "power of positive force,"

"creative mind" and "best efforts" can bring about unbelievable results. I have selected several episodes from them. ▲ Book 1 deals with my own confessions on the topic of creative best efforts from the perspective of a person working as a patent attorney. ▲ Book 2 deals with the behind-the-scenes story of how an established Supreme Court case is reversed and a new precedent is adopted and relied upon. I have also added the applicable court decisions to give better context.

I am reminded over and over again that the secret to happiness is confronting and overcoming adversities even where creative best efforts did not appear adequate. Even at our firm, which celebrated its 20th anniversary last fall, there are many areas where sweat and effort of our team laid the foundation on which the passion and commitment of our work is based.

First experience is heart-pounding electricity. When challenged by my life's twists and turns, I held tightly unto the hand of my "Almighty God" and faced them without running away. My first dance at an international conference, my first presentation before an international audience, my first chairmanship at an international conference, my first book publication, my first university lecture and my first appearance as a TV talk show host were all adventurous undertakings for me.

My memories of those first experiences where I took the challenge without cowering are still fresh in my mind. What followed those first experiences energized and excited me as I looked forward to the fruits of my labor. I am eager to tell my grandkids of my own sense of achievements through these experiences.

I also want to share my personal realization of unique and dazzling experiences of "creative best efforts" not only with my peer patent attorneys, but also with all other professionals, business people and my good neighbors on this planet.

I am grateful to my close friend and former colleague Andrew S. Kim, Esq., for his time and effort in translating this book into plain and easy-to-read English.

Lastly, I dedicate this book in warm loving memory of my wife Jungsook Julie.

January 2017

Ho Hyun Nahm
Lead Partner
BARUN IP & LAW

BOOK 1

Power of Positive Force

CAST YOUR NET ON THE DEEP SIDE

-Power of the positive

"… man does not live on bread alone but on every word that comes from the mouth of the Lord." (Deuteronomy 8:3).

This bible verse is the truth of the truth. The power of this positive message is a widely-known truth, and reciting this passage rattles my heart and awakens me every time. I also have three other verses that have governed my life and led me to who I am today.

"God is Almighty… (2 Maccabees 8:18)"

"… Put out into deep water, and let down the nets for a catch. (Luke 5:4)"

"… a prophet has no honor in his own country. (John 4:44)"

I was born in the deepest mountain and the most rural countryside village called Sangchon in Youngdong-gun, Choongchung province, known for great mountains and clean water. My family was poor. I lost my father at such an early age that I don't remember what he looked like. I was able to grow up only with the loving care from my mother and my older brother. While they provided me with the material necessities to live and grow, they gave me something of infinitely more value - they allowed me to get to know God.

At the time, my older brother was attending Sungeui High School in Kimchun where Cardinal Soohwan Kim (then, a priest) served as the school principal. With the consent of my then-living father at the time, my brother introduced Catholicism to our family. My mother became deeply religious and even served as the head of the church congregation. As a result, I received

3

the honor of being baptized as an infant. I had been baptized regardless of my will.

When I became of elementary school age and learned a little bit of the church doctrines, I received Communion and Confirmation. In those days, mass was conducted in Latin, and not in Korean. Although I did not know what they all meant, I nevertheless memorized all of the Latin words. Exchanging prayers in Latin with the priest and practicing for the mass are part of my beautiful memory of those days.

The teaching that continued to govern my life from my youth days was "God is Almighty." In my junior high, high school and college years, "Back-up" was a widely-used word to describe the social environment then. "Back-up" is a slang term for an acquaintance or sponsor with some authority that provides support for a person. In fact, our society was quite irrational in those days where someone lacking merit but with a strong "Back-up" would readily find path to success whereas someone with merit but without any "Back-up" would not even be given the time of day. But I had the most powerful and reliable "Back-up" in the world - the Almighty God.

Similar to electricity where power is obtained by plugging the cord into an outlet, I believed that everything was possible as long as I held tightly on to the hand of the Almighty God. That's why I was able to dream as big as I did even though I didn't have any other person teaching me the ways of the world. I truly believed that anything was possible as long as I held the Almighty God's hand.

Nothing really intimidated me. I didn't have a father; my family was stricken with extreme poverty; I was living in the most remote rural village separated from the outside world - nonetheless, I was a confident kid. Even among friends, I never felt inferior in any respects. I was bold, which allowed me to be unique and do what I wanted without hesitation. At a time when it was unheard of for a student to wear "hanbok" (traditional Korean costume) to school, I proudly wore the top and bottom "hanbok," which my mother made by herself to keep me warm during winter, to school. I had the Almight God's "Back-up."

Without the Almighty God, it would have been impossible for me to be bold enough to pester my teacher to give me the role of the king in a school play and to enjoy oratory from elementary school to high school. Every twist and turn in my life, my Almighty God was the reliable "Back-up" I needed.

From a government employee (at the time, Foreign Public Relations officer of the Ministry of Culture and Information) to an employee of a conglomerate (a member of the legal team at Korean Air), and then to patent attorney, I was able to continue to transform and progress only because God had always been with me. The wonderful godly experiences are too many to repeat.

Maccabees once told his soldiers:

"They rely on their weapons and their daring, but we trust in Almighty God, who is able to destroy not only these troops, but, if necessary, the entire world, with a mere nod of his head."

Even now, I believe that my Almighty God's unwavering "Back-up" is enabling me to have the ability to complete this book even while hospitalized.

When I was young, I dreamed of becoming a priest and working actively in the international scene. While I gave up on the priesthood after meeting "Jungsook Julie," my wife and the love of my life, I still take pride in the fact that I was able to achieve my dream of working actively in the international scene.

I firmly believed it, and I wanted to believe it as well - that our society would evolve into the "intellectual information society" and that patent attorneys who have a critical role in the intellectual information society would become one of its most pivotal professions. I took the patent attorney examination, considered at the time to be a herculean task, and passed. That was a period in which only one or two, and sometimes none, passed the examination for the whole year. What made it possible for me to even dare taking the patent attorney examination was because I believed in my Almighty God's "Back-up."

After I became a patent attorney, I decided to leave Korean Air, my employer at the time. I boldly decided to leave Lee & Ko (also Gwang Jang

Law Firm) where I had helped to start the patent department and served as the department's inaugural general manager. I then transferred to Central International Patent and Law Firm, which was at the time the largest patent law firm in Korea, to take my first step as a patent attorney.

"… a prophet has no honor in his own country. (John 4:44)"

My heart absorbed these words of Jesus like a wet sponge. As is true with most professional occupations, the power of a professional comes from the clients. And one of the most critical elements to the success of a professional is how well person acquires clients.

In our country, the so-called "Back-up" still plays a major role, including relationships based on one's family, where one is from or what school one attended. Although I graduated from a regional university, and not a nationally-recognized prestigious university, I did have some pretty significant school-based relationships. But it definitely wasn't as good as someone from a prestigious university. I was also facing a biased perception that a professional who graduated from a prestigious university is likely to be more qualified or competitive than one from a regional university. I wanted to tear down that wall of bias.

DANCING AT MY FIRST INTERNATIONAL CONFERENCE

Jesus said, "… put out into deep water, and let down the nets for a catch. (Luke 5:4)"

"Master, we've worked hard all night and haven't caught anything. But because you say so, I will let down the nets." Disciple Simon does as Jesus says. They then catch such a large number of fish that their nets begin to break. They motion their partners in the other boat to come and help them, and they came and helped bring the catch aboard. The catch fills both boats which are so full that they began to sink. How much more exhilarating can a story get than this?

Wanting to cast my net on the deep side, I turned my eyes toward the international law practice. Yes, let's go to the deep side. I decided to venture into the "Blue Ocean" where they don't discriminate merely because you are from a regional university.

The primary arena for a patent attorney is in the intellectual property area which includes patents, designs and trademarks, and these areas involve creation and protection of rights that are independently acquired for each country, and as a result, international protection is one which is critically necessary for any holder of such rights.

For this reason, foreign companies have no choice but to apply for and register their trademarks and patents in our country in order to conduct business here. Even though I had only joined Central International Patent and Law Firm as a rookie patent attorney for just a few months, I was assigned to attend a major international conference by myself.

It was about 30 years ago. My first entrance into the international scene. My heart pounded. This was my first overseas trip as well. My first conference was called USTA (Annual Meeting of the United States Trademark Association). It was held in the City of Phoenix, State of Arizona. At the time, this conference was attended by about 1,500 trademark professionals, including those from U.S. as well as around the world. This conference has since changed its name to INTA (International Trademark Association) and has transformed into a colossal international conference, bringing together about 10,000 trademark-related professionals each year.

Watching experts from other countries give presentations on specific topics inspired me to do the same someday. But this was easier said than done. You couldn't even fathom this happening unless you spoke highly proficient English, let alone have the requisite expertise in the area to be able to give an international perspective to other professionals in the field.

But I didn't think that was impossible. I just needed to hold on to the Almighty God's hand. By the way, didn't I already have pretty good oratory skills? I tried to encourage myself in many ways, but just trying to understand the contents of the presentations was challenging enough for me at the time due to the language barrier.

I also went on interesting tours while there. For me, even a rodeo show with a bunch of cowboys was a pretty unique spectacle. But what is this? It was just like a countryside boy visiting Seoul. Each day, there were special events, including the opening ceremony, private receptions, farewell parties and the like, as well as all the great food and drink one can consume. There were parties where people were dressed in their own traditional costumes and dancing to the music. I just didn't know where to keep my eyes.

At my first meeting, I sat with participants from various other countries. A woman attorney from Australia and another one from Finland, a male patent attorney from Singapore – they all sat stone-faced and were watching the festivities. So I decided to get up.

"Let's all dance!"

Although I said it, I didn't know how to dance. I certainly didn't know how to dance like the people on the dance floor. Where did I get the nerve to tell people to get up and dance? Yes, the Almighty God. Everybody at first politely refused. They said that they didn't know how to dance… So I boldly told them.

"Do you know what dance is? It's just moving with music. Formality and rules may be important, but isn't just moving your body with the music the most natural way to dance?"

Everybody cheered and began to dance. While dancing with me, the woman attorney from Finland said "let's not stop!"

We danced well over 1 am. Most of the friends I met that night have turned into mutual clients with whom I exchange work until this day. Looking back, I am grateful for my first experience that night as it bestowed on me many gifts for a long time.

After the conference, I decided to visit Grand Canyon National Park while returning home. I remembered Mr. Chun Deuk Pi's "Coming Back from Grand Canyon," which I read in our junior high Korean language textbook. I made a reservation on a light aircraft to fly to Nevada from Los Angeles.

"I'm curious about your weight."

A lady who appeared to be pretty slim herself came and asked me for my weight.

"Why is she concerned about weight when getting on a plane?"

I cast my suspicious look on her in response. To my surprise, she was the pilot for the 7-people light aircraft. To me, she looked like a bus attendant back home. Even worse, rather than focusing on piloting the plane, she was busy trying to keep the passengers occupied, such as "look left!", "look right!", "look below!", "look there!", "how do you feel?"

All of a sudden, I felt like we were dropping straight down 100 meters. Everybody probably got a little airsick. After landing in an airport in Nevada, the driver of the car awaiting me was also a young lady.

"Women are truly working in all areas of the job market in the U.S."

I was impressed, and it reminded me of how our country remains to be extremely conservative and how limited the options are for women to enter the working world in Korea. Finally, we are close to Grand Canyon, one that epitomizes God's creative spirit. Wow, I can't help but let out a scream in delight.

A great and boundless portrait of valleys unfolded before my eyes. Its reddish-lighted raw figures are fully revealed. Its gigantic and imposing grandeur continues endlessly. Intimidating-looking cliffs, multi-colored layers of earth, sharp and high rugged mountains and numerous fantastically-shaped rocks are further complemented by the Colorado River underneath, all of which combine to produce an unforgettable grand view. The walls of the valleys which are as high as 1,500 meters reflect the numerous earth strata that have formed for 20 billion years since the Archeozoic Era.

While admiring everything in sight, I walked along the South Rim that runs along one side of the river. For the first time, I also enjoyed Grand Canyon through an IMAX movie as well. Similar to my feelings when I later visited Niagara Fall, I felt in my heart the power of the Creator's omniscience and omnipotence. I truly believe that my first overseas trip to such a fantastic destination was a planned blessing from the Almighty God.

I prepared and submitted a detailed report of the business trip to Mr. Byong Ho Lee, the Senior Partner of Central International Patent and Law Firm. He seemed very satisfied. And then, something amazing started to happen. The friends I had made during my first overseas business trip began to send cases to our firm! I was ecstatic. This development served as the impetus for Mr. Byong Ho Lee to designate me to attend international conferences and business trips on a regular basis. Countless foreign travels followed. So many trips…

Now, almost without exception, I attend INTA meetings, which was my first international conference, as well as Pharmaceutical Trademarks Group (PTMG), European Communities Trademark Association (ECTA), the Association Internationale pour la Protection de la Propriete (AIPPI), Federation Internationale Des Conseils En Propriete Intellectuelle (FICPI) and Asian Patent Attorneys Association (APAA) on their annual meetings, board meetings and open forums. Since these meetings are held in different locations throughout the world, it has essentially allowed me to travel to almost all of the world's best attractions.

MY FIRST BOOK PUBLICATION

-Sharing the topic of intellectual property with the public-

"When shared, joy multiplies."

This is an old proverb from Spain. As a specialist in intellectual property, I do possess some valuable experience and expertise in this area. What is the true value of an intellectual property and what can qualify as intellectual property? What is necessary to create intellectual property, and how can someone acquire rights in it and not lose them? As an expert in this area, I was able to achieve a certain level of experience and expertise. That's good news for me.

I wanted to share the good news with the general public. So I decided to write a book - a book containing fundamental principles of intellectual property rights. I must have written about 100 pages, and it dawned on me that this book, when published, would find its way to the bookshelves of some experts and then would be forgotten.

"Yes, why am I writing something that experts already know about? I should write a book that is entertaining and easy to read for the general public who may be aware of the importance of intellectual property rights but don't have a way to understand them more easily."

Having changed my mind, I set out to write a book with a different approach. I didn't realize, however, how difficult it was to write a book that the general public could readily relate to, especially since intellectual property was an area that even experts in the field, including patent attorneys and attorneys, consider to be a challenging topic. This undertaking required much greater creative effort than simply writing about the fundamental principles and theories.

The general public would perceive intellectual property rights and intellectual property law as boring, difficult and hard to understand. How can I make it fun for them to read? After much deliberation, I decided to write about my own story. Not just any story, but one that a reader can connect naturally to better understand intellectual property rights.

I believed that it would be natural for readers to become absorbed in the world of intellectual property rights through personal anecdotes. I can begin by writing about how I lived as a youngster, how I became a patent attorney and what a patent attorney does. I can then introduce all areas of intellectual property rights, including patents, trademarks, designs, utility models, copyrights, computer programs, domain names and trade secrets, and the basic practical knowledge useful for the general public in the form of fun and entertaining storytelling style like Aesop's.

For example, to explain the required element of "novelty" for registering a patent, I used the Chapter title "Waving One's Hand After The Bus Departs" and introduced an actual case that I handled on this issue using a pamphlet that was distributed prior to the filing of the patent.

In explaining the required element of "distinctiveness" in trademarks, I told my own "love story" between a buzz-cut, bespectacled junior high school kid and a beautiful American English teacher. "The Chef Who Stole the Secret Recipe of 'Ih-dong Galbi'" was the title I used to illustrate the law on protection of trade secrets. The manuscript for the book was finally completed.

The book became a much more polished work after my close friend, Sunggil Kim who is a writer, proofread and edited it. I needed to find a publisher. Thinking that this book needed to be properly marketed to be successful, I went to Chosun Daily Newspaper as they had a good reputation in book publishing. Without hesitation, they agreed to publish. They proposed the title,

"Challenging the 21ˢᵗ Century with Intellectual Property Rights," since we were about to enter the new century. I requested that the cover page feature my photo because I wanted to make sure that I was communicating my special message to the general public.

Through articles and advertising, Chosun Daily Newspaper did a good job of marketing the book, as I had hoped. It became a bestseller in the category of Economy/Management with Kyobo Bookstore, and it also was designated as a recommended reading for teenagers. I take much pride in this book. The fact that there were many readers, including people preparing for the patent attorney examination and teenagers, who actually read this book was proof that my driving force and creative method of delivering fun and engaging stories to tell the difficult topic of intellectual property and related laws actually worked as I had envisioned. For this, I am much grateful.

This book was later adapted into a new book under the title of "Everything Under The Sun Can Be Patented," which was published and sold by Yega Publishing Company. It was also published in English and Japanese versions. I have also given this book as a complementary gift to a lot of my friends overseas after personally signing it. In addition to receiving their words of appreciation, nothing makes me more happy to know that I was able to introduce the Korean intellectual property system to all parts of the global world through fun and interesting stories.

With anything, once a path is cleared, it is easier to expand and travel on that path. My desire to write more books just got started.

"The source of intellectual property lies in invention. But it's not only the complex and grand technology that makes money or becomes intellectual property. Even a simple and humble idea or the fruit of a wife's love and neighbor's consideration can lead to a substantial intellectual property."

To encourage and inspire inventive efforts, I put together about 40 fun stories involving actual cases. This was the book entitled "Change Your Life with An Idea," which was published through Park Young Books. Also, a good friend of mine from U.K., who is also a well-known patent attorney there, told me that he wanted to have his book "From Edison to iPad" revised to conform to Korean laws and published in our language. With me as a co-author! Work on this book has been completed to reflect applicable Korean laws, and publication will take place soon.

I received a request from INTA, my first international conference and one which boasts of tens of thousands of members from all over the world. They said that they are compiling a book on the law and procedure on the topic of trademark opposition in each country and that they wanted me to prepare its Korean Chapter. Of course, I accepted without hesitation.

This book is now a part of **INTA** International Trademark Association the International Opposition Guide (http://www.inta.org/Oppositions/Pages/IOG.aspx), and it is available on INTA's official website to anyone seeking information on the trademark opposition of any member country. Recently, I completed the Korean Chapter of **INTA** International Trademark Association Enforcement _ An International Litigation Guide (http://www.inta.org/EnforcementGuides/Pages/EnforcementGuides.aspx), which INTA asked me to write. In late 2015, Oxford University Press published a highly authoritative book entitled "Domain Name Law and Practice _ An International Handbook," for which I wrote its Korean Chapter.

I am extremely happy to share my experience and expertise on intellectual property with people from all parts of the world. I am living proof that a person, whether a professional or a non-professional, should express their intellectual possessions in a creative form and leave a written record for the benefit of common use. It will shine permanently and have an immortal value.

MY FIRST UNIVERSITY LECTURE

It was about 17 years ago, and it must have been the result of my humble book. A fellow patent attorney and at the time a law professor of Sookmyung Women's University called me. He asked that I teach a course on "intellectual property law," an elective course on campus. Without hesitation, I accepted.

This was a special course, open to freshmen to seniors. I put tremendous effort into making this course as interesting as possible based on my book "Challenging the 21st Century with Intellectual Property Rights." I had no idea about the joy I would feel in transferring my knowledge to wide-eyed and vivacious young women listening attentively to my lectures.

After the final exam, we held a farewell party. Almost all of the students in the class came. It was very satisfying. Since I know my alcohol limit, I offered and accepted a drink to each of them. I ended up reaching my limit.

Three or four hours had passed. I tried to get up, thinking it was time to go. What happens? Two students came out of nowhere and linked arms with me. I was a little startled.

"Professor, are you leaving? Where? You cannot go. From now on, we'll guide you."

I'm in trouble. I've already filled my alcohol limit, but there are still eight students left here. They took me to a traditional Korean pub. Then they want to play a drinking game? Well, they called it a game, but it was a big conspiracy. The drink was dongdongju (rice wine). Complimentary side dish was pajeon (green onion pancake), my favorite. Eight young female university students surrounded me and became the life of the party. With so much fun, I went overboard and drank way beyond my alcohol limit.

Is there anyone in the world, including any King, that has ever received such attention and service from pure, well-intentioned, beautiful female university students who provided all the fun and wasn't expecting anything in return? I came home after 3 am that night, soaked in alcohol.

To make things worse, my mother had come to our house for a visit. I was told that she was very worried. Next morning, she made a hearty breakfast with bean sprouts soup for me and made sure to caution me to "act properly!" That was the first time I received a motherly reprimand about alcohol from her. I did hear her message, but I am keeping that sweet memory from my first university lecture experience near and dear to my heart for a long time.

I received another request for lecture on intellectual property law, this time from Korean National Police University. I gladly accepted with the notion that the police officers who are on the frontline of law enforcement need to be knowledgeable about intellectual property law. I devised a different method of teaching than the one I used at Sookmyung Women's University since they needed to accurately understand the related laws in order to enjoy any practical benefits in real situations.

I prepared a PowerPoint presentation of all of the intellectual property law areas, including patent law, utility model law, design protection law, trademark law, unfair competition prevention law, law on protection of trade secrets, copyright law, and resolution of disputes on Internet domain names. I wanted the police officer candidates to easily, efficiently and accurately understand the most critical areas of these laws in a short semester. Having lectured to attentive and bright-eyed university students who will eventually serve as high-ranking officers on the national police scene, I took comfort in the bright future of our country that they will soon represent.

After the final exam, I suggested a farewell party, which was well received by the students. Most everyone attended, even though I understand farewell parties are no longer in fashion. My friend who is a professor at this school and who arranged for me to teach at the Korean National Police University grumbled, "we have a problem because some of our best students now want to become patent attorneys instead of police officers, and it's because of you!"

Although both Sookmyung Women's University and the Korean National Police University asked me to continue to teach, it just was not easy. My frequent overseas business trips required me to miss classes and in turn this placed tremendous unfair burden on the students. As a result, I had no choice but to discontinue my lectures.

I guess the word got around, and I was receiving many requests for lectures. If I had the best interests of my firm's international business in mind, I would have had to refuse them all. But I thought that there was better value in spreading and educating the message about intellectual property law to the public at large. As long as the schedule didn't conflict with my overseas business trips, I tried to accept as many requests as I possibly could.

Wherever possible, whether at domestic and international symposiums and seminars, the Constitutional Court, Seoul National University, Ministry of Government Administration and Home Affairs, Korea Attorneys Association, the Federation of Korean Industries, or even remote local regional governments as well as major conglomerates, I made presentations on the importance of intellectual property and the ways in which to acquire and exercise such rights. Although I had to split my precious time to do this, I found them to be extremely rewarding.

My beloved grandkids, I hope that you can likewise find joy in life by sharing your possessions with the society. You will most certainly discover paradise in your heart and soul.

FIRST TV APPEARANCE AS A TALK SHOW HOST

Again, another bonus from the popularity of my book. Maeil Economic Daily's TV station, Maeil Broadcasting Network (MBN), sent me a proposal to host a program on intellectual property rights. I was told the content of the program should center around the materials contained in my book. But, they're asking this not just for a single show, but multiple shows - once a week for six months! I was dumbfounded. But, like before, I accepted the proposal in reliance of the Almighty God. Shooting this program took me to so many different locations.

The story of "the Chef Who Stole the Secret Recipe of 'Ih-dong Galbi'" was shot in the Chungmuro restaurant district, which is near to my office at the time. People nearby started to gather and whispered, hoping to catch a glimpse of a well-known actor.

I saw my first TV show. The program was entitled, "Ho Hyun Nahm's Fun Patent Stories." I was too stiff and dry. But then again, once a path is paved, the next travel gets easier. I improved from repetition. Although I obviously lacked skills as a TV show host, I was once again immensely happy to have reached the general public with basic information and stories on intellectual property through television.

I also appeared as a guest on various radio shows including "MBC's Invitation" hosted by Simin Yoo, a former congressman and "Hello, this is Banghee Kim" hosted by a veteran broadcaster Banghee Kim. My message was being transmitted to every nook and cranny of the land through television and radio media. Those who saw or heard my broadcasts may not remember my name. But it nevertheless gives me much satisfaction to think that the interesting stories I passed along may serve as a seed for better understanding of intellectual property.

MY FIRST PRESENTATION AT AN INTERNATIONAL CONFERENCE

In 2004, I received a proposal to give a presentation from the Vice Chairman of Pharmaceutical Trade Marks Group. I am asked to give an hour-long presentation to discuss the trademark systems for six Asian countries, including Korea. There will be about 500 participants in attendance from various countries. I felt helpless. I had never given a presentation in English to an international audience. Fear gripped me a little. But I told her that I would do it.

I started collecting information for the presentation by contacting my friends in the other countries. Then, I began working on developing an impressive powerpoint slide show. At that time, there was no one on staff at our office who was skilled in preparing powerpoint. I hired an outside specialist to design the powerpoint the way I wanted to use it. Once the materials were ready, I practiced and practiced. I pretty much memorized the entire presentation.

The day of reckoning is coming soon. I once again rehearse my presentation in the hotel room the night before. Somebody then knocks on my door. The person staying next door requests that he "be allowed to sleep." I guess I was practicing too loudly as if I was in an oratorical contest in my younger days. Embarrassed, I apologize to the person next door and crash to sleep.

Finally, the presentation day arrived. I kept thinking, how can I impress my audience and capture their emotion and attention? I chose to use my experiences from oratory background in my school days. Make changes in the presentation to change the tone, adjust the trajectory of my voice and insert humor where appropriate. I decide to do my presentation centered around one of the stories in my book "Challenging the 21st Century with Intellectual Property Rights" as published by Chosun Daily Newspaper.

The story was a passage from the chapter entitled "Dazzling Distinctiveness." It was a story about my teacher who gave me special attention by asking me many questions, remembering my name, engaging me in conversations during breaks, selecting me to participate in a English speech competition and correcting my pronunciation.

The story of my beautiful teacher, Ms. Jane Jones. She had come to our school as one of the members of the US Peace Corps and was volunteering as an English teacher.

"Wow, I think this beautiful teacher likes me."

It was enough to shake an 8th grader's fluttering heart. In an effort to impress her even more, I studied English like crazy. I would often memorize the entire textbook and then I would boastfully show off. One day, I finally asked her why she was showing a special interest in me and was being so kind to me. Her response was classic.

"It's not that you are smarter or cuter than others. You are different from other kids because you wear glasses. I can recognize you better because of your glasses."

I listened attentively to my teacher's confession.

"I had no way of telling who's who in class because everyone has a buzz-cut and everyone wears the black school uniform. But I could tell you apart from others with ease because you wore glasses."

Although this quickly crushed any slim chance that she had a crush on me, I did benefit greatly from my glasses. I was able to receive private lessons from Ms. Jones to improve my pronunciation, and as a result, I learned to be confident when speaking English with a foreigner. I was a lucky guy.

"This is what you call distinctiveness in trademarks. Now, I will introduce each country's system on trademark distinctiveness."

This story received a good laughter from the audience, and they gave me a loud applause when I finished. My first virgin presentation to an international audience was a success. Once this path was paved, various international organizations invited me to speak at their events. I truly enjoyed my experiences in giving presentations on a variety of subjects at these meetings.

My most memorable presentation was the one I gave at INTA (formerly USTA) at its Berlin Meetings. This is the organization whose event I attended for my first international conference and where I started to dream about giving a presentation. I finally realized that dreams will come true even if you may not be aware of it. I am listing my international presentations in the appendix of this book.

MY FIRST CHAIRMANSHIP AT AN INTERNATIONAL CONFERENCE

Fear took over when I was offered the chairmanship of the trademark committee of Asian Patent Attorneys Association. That was because it involved chairing a three-hour marathon meeting with over 50 representatives from 24 member countries.

While there were English - speaking member countries, such as from Australia, Singapore and Hong Kong, most other member countries were non-English speaking. As such, the problem for me was going to be trying to understand the unique accents of participants from the non-English speaking countries when they speak English. I dwelled on it for a few days, but I ended up accepting the offered role.

In my first year as the chairman of the trademark committee, I pursued two types of reforms. The topic for the meeting can largely be divided into two categories. One was the reporting of and discussion on the developments of each country's trademark system and relevant case law. The other was the report and discussion on special topics. In prior meetings, the representatives from 24 countries would simply come up and read their respective reports. Frankly, it was boring and unproductive. Requests by the executive committee for participants to read the reports prior to the meeting and engage in follow-up questions and discussions were largely ignored.

I wanted to enforce this policy strictly. To do this, I, as the chairman, had to read all of the reports from each country and be familiar with all of the critical issues prior to the meeting. If no one raised any questions, I had to ask the appropriate questions to keep the discussions flowing. As a result, the representatives from each country came to the meeting prepared and the discussion became lively. The meeting was no longer boring, and it moved very efficiently.

But the special topics portion was different. In prior meetings, organizers would simply designate the special topic, and each representative presented their reports without organization and focus. Getting this back in order was indeed a daunting task.

In response, I developed a matrix. Every time a special topic was designated, ten sub-topics were also designated. I made participants answer each sub-topic as positive or negative, or neither, and also to submit personal comments. This was prepared prior to the meeting, and all participants were required to submit a report based on the information reflected on the matrix. It allowed a clearer understanding of the system related to special topic presentations, and the discussions became more focused.

I enjoyed serving two 3-years terms for a total of 6 years. I take special pride in seeing that the meetings are now organized based on my two reforms. I also was able to learn a valuable experience which validated the fact that there is great value in making efforts to find creative solutions over maintaining obsolete and inefficient processes.

THE CREATIVE MINORITY'S RESPONSE TO CHALLENGE

Anyone can become a creative minority that leads a civilization. Arnold Toynbee is a scholar who devoted his life to the study of history. In his work, "A Study of History," a 12-volume piece which took him 27 years to complete, he wrote,

"Civilizations grow only when environment and life are challenged and they respond to those challenges, and those who respond to challenges are 'Creative Minorities'."

Generally, a leader of a society would fit this description. But the problem is that all leaders are not necessarily "Creative Minorities." A creative leader who opens a new path is a creative minority who responds to meet the challenges to a civilization. Surprisingly, however, we see that creative minority often descends into a "dominant minority." Toynbee proclaims,

"In that case, a new creative minority rises and responds to challenges, leading the civilization to grow."

Toynbee observes civilization from a macro perspective, and in his eyes, his mother is a creative minority. In other words, anyone can be a creative minority. I would like to think that this concept applies even to a small community of even two people.

One thing that is clear is that it must not descend into a dominant minority. Whether our country's leaders are actually creative minorities or creative minorities who descended into dominant minorities is a question that most people in-the-know readily know and doesn't require history critics of future generations to analyze.

We need to think and think again about creative ideas and creative core. If one person in any family qualified as a creative minority, that family and household are in good hands. Any small group or company will undoubtedly grow if its parts or divisions endeavor to become the creative minority. Managers or team leaders aren't the only ones who can be creative minorities. How dull would life be if we simply continued to work the same way and do the same thing we have always done? Changing day by day represents true life.

My grandkids, don't just continue to do things the old way, whether it's with your group of friends or in an organization you belong to. Take all aspects of that organization, from product manufacturing process, designs, sales methods to service methods, and rethink creatively from the beginning. And communicate… effectively. You can be a leader of the creative minority by engaging in effective communication even if you are not in a leadership role as a manager, team leader or supervisor.

Putting aside monetary rewards, how delightful would it be to witness the change and growth of your own group or society through creative ideas? We must not refuse the opportunity to proclaim ourselves as a creative minority and offer our services to others. In some ways, the process by which we become creative minorities is one of our holy obligations.

PARTICIPATING IN KING'S COURT

It is a common sense that science, technology and invention serve as the engine for a country's growth and driving force. The period of ignorance and brutality where one country invades and occupies another to expand their borders is over.

By arming ourselves with patent rights that confer monopoly rights on science, technology and invention, we can expand our economic borders beyond Korea and into U.S., China, Europe and wherever patent rights are acquired. Similar to the consequences for invading our country's borders, if someone were to infringe on our exclusive patent rights, we can respond by filing for injunction against infringement and damages.

We no longer honor war heroes as much as we do sports heroes or heroes of technology and invention. The leaders of intellectual property in areas of new and advanced technology and invention, creative literature, design and branding should be considered the true heroes of our time.

Is there a new path that takes us out of our routines? Is there a new way? Think and think again. Not just casually. Do it with all your might, and do it with passion, earnest and joy. Trust that when you put out your "creative best effort," you can be transformed into an intellectual property hero and creative minority that will lead this generation.

To bring about a successful technology development and invention in terms of expanding our national territory, creating a national support structure in the form of government planning and budget allocation is critical. This approach is in fact the only practical pathway to expanding our borders, and it also governs the issue of competitive survival for our nation. As such, I believe that there is a more urgent need to allocate an appropriate budget towards this end than that allocated towards national defense. That is because there is more than adequate value there.

Whether the technology relates to electrical engineering, mechanical engineering or bioengineering, technology advancements not only bring benefit to the people of our country but contribute to the advancement of welfare of all humanity.

From this vantage point, I applaud the installation of "Presidential Advisory Council on Science & Technology" that serves as an advisory group to the President with the President as its chairman pursuant to our Constitution.

"Almost all policy comes from the President Advisory Council. For this Council to have proper representation, I don't think that it's good to reduce the number of advisors in the Council."

President Moo Hyun Roh announced on October 20, 2005. On the same day, President Roh held a meeting of the Presidential Advisory Council on Science & Technology at Cheongwadae (Blue House) and said the following:

"I think that a government that utilizes the most number of advisory boards probably better fits the description of the Participatory Government (a nick name of President Roh Government). Recently, I find wealth of success in the science and technology field."

I remember with honor and fondness to have been appointed as an advisor to the Presidential Advisory Council on Science & Technology in 2005 and serving in its 9th advisory group. After personally receiving the Certificate of Appointment from President Roh on October 20, 2005, I attended the meeting of the science and technology council presided by the President on the topic of "Strengthening the Competitive Edge for Small and Medium-Sized Enterprises'Technology Utilizing Government Research Institutions." In the old days, this would have been the King's Court.

I was not one of the presenters that day, but I quickly realized how exceptionally analytical and insightful President Roh was. Having already understood the presentation materials, President Roh said the following:

"Weren't these discussions already presented before? Those others appear to be new materials, but additional research should be done since they are not supported by data or empirical evidence."

His remarks were truly astute. President Roh praised the current state of the level of Korea's science and technology and did not hold back his praise and encouragement for those in this field. In his address, President Roh emphasized :

There are things that go well and things that do not. But we are seeing good results from the science and technology fields, and for this, I am likewise delighted. While we still have some shortcomings in all areas, the results are generally good which also makes me feel good. Let's all try to work even harder.

President Roh continued with his address :

I am so proud of our scientists. I'm not sure if it is still considered a threat for a son to tell his dad that he wants to major in science and engineering, but if the scientists keep this up, we will soon see a time when kids will say that their dream and hope are to become scientists.

After handing out the Certificate of Appointments to the appointed advisory members of the Presidential Advisory Council on Science & Technology, President Roh talked about the reasons for increasing the number of advisory members from ten to thirty :

The Korean society has become so much more diverse, multi-dimensional and profound that reducing the number of advisory members for the sake of authority is not good, especially if the Council is to be composed of representative authorities in their respective disciplines. The number may seem large, but it is really not when considering the diversity.

I took a picture alone with the President. The gifts bearing the Presidential seal I receive on national holidays are overwhelming. I considered his policy of prioritizing science and technology to be a part of the process as a creative minority, and for that, I found President Roh's creative best efforts to be a beautiful undertaking. I will consider that to be deeply meaningful.

Likewise, President Keun-Hye Park also emphasizes creative economy whenever the opportunity is presented, including her chairmanship of the Presidential Advisory Council on Science & Technology. However, China is catching up with our country's technical competence in electronics. Bioengineering is the new hot ticket and one that we clearly need to pursue. Despite that, the reality is that there just isn't enough investment in this area because of the enormous investment it requires and an even longer road to return on investment. Because of that, even the Samsung Group is unable to commit the necessary resources in this area.

The government must identify a reliable industry that can serve as the engine for future growth - one that is beyond any given company's own resources. There must be sufficient support from the government to entice private companies to commit their investment.

ROYAL TREATMENT BY A FOREIGN COMPANY

When visiting a foreign multinational corporation overseas, I am treated to a red carpet treatment. If the visit is in the morning, they generally treat me to lunch either in a VIP room at their company cafeteria or at a fancy restaurant outside. A full course meal, from appetizer to dessert, takes place. A glass of wine is common and the dessert menu is magnificent.

In this environment, I prefer cognac that goes well with dessert. Generally, official meeting and discussions take place at the office. Equally helpful in understanding work and building trust and relationship is the couple of hours spent over a meal talking about this and that.

There's more. Some clients provide use of their company's luxury limousine to take me to my next meeting, hotel or to the airport. Even I find myself deeply impressed as I ride alone in a limousine that is almost as long as a bus, taking out a cold beer from the refrigerator inside the limousine while being driven from New Jersey to my hotel in Manhattan. It's true that anyone can ride in a limousine if they pay for it. But it makes it all more thrilling to be treated to this luxury by the host multinational company.

What happens after receiving such generous hospitality? We may be working at a foreign location away from the client, but we are fully integrated as one with our client. In other words, we naturally become a loyal part of the client. From the client's perspective, it makes sense to be generously hospitable so that the foreign counsel can feel like a close family. This mindset and process lead the foreign counsel to work genuinely in the best interest of the client.

This is where we can think hard about the mentality of some of the conglomerates in our country who routinely squeeze their vendor companies to accept lower prices, who are ready to disqualify them on the finding of any error and who do not pay timely when due. Why is that? It's because they see vendor companies as third parties, and not as a part of their company.

Why do they not realize that the employees of their vendor companies are the same as their employees? Would they sustain and grow as a company without the blood, sweat and tears of those employees? It is said that love should have no conditions attached, but one good turn deserves another. Our future will be bright if the executives and employees of conglomerates start to give due consideration to the welfare and well-being of the employees of their vendor companies.

Research analysis and data show that creative ideas and outstanding inventions come more from smaller-sized companies or individuals as opposed to conglomerates. Smaller units of organizations combine to form large ones. No one should look down on someone because of size. While our society may have grown somewhat materially, the level of our moral culture still has a long way to go. Let's not forget that. We must not forget that individuals and small-sized companies are the lifeline and progress for the conglomerates and are the starting and destination point for the creative best effort and creative minority.

VOLUNTEER WORK AS A CREATIVE MINORITY

Unexpectedly, I was elected unanimously as the President of the Korean Chapter of the Asia Patent Attorneys Association. I now proudly claim that I was able to achieve significant results in terms of improving the rights and interests of the members from my creative best efforts during my tenure. This is reflected in the active level of participation of the next generation of Korean patent attorneys, and for this, I am profoundly happy. The following is my address given at the General Meeting in 2015 Spring after having completed my three-year term as the President of Asia Patent Attorneys Association.

"Dear honorable members, three years have already passed since I was elected as the 11th President. Three years ago, I revealed to you my vision of elevating our Association into a greater organization with character and charisma from the beautifully-developed garden cultivated with solidarity and hard work from my predecessors.

I remember running for the presidency of our Chapter with the motto of "Charismatic APAA Korea" in an effort to contribute, in my own humble way, to make that vision become a reality and to reconstruct and reshape our Chapter.

As the first step towards "Charismatic APAA Korea," I put my heart and soul into forming a charismatic group of individuals for our executive committee. With the solidarity of all such charismatic officers on our executive committee, we really worked diligently to make our Chapter the "Charismatic APAA Korea" by working to achieve the ten objectives that I promised I would pursue if elected President three years ago: fortify better relationship and welfare, expand rights and interests beyond friendly relationships, increase membership and attain internal stability, strengthen APAA Korea's role within APAA International, generate more international network, increase support for participating in international events by members, strengthen cooperation with related organizations, help form more workshops with APAA International, pursue committee participation and cooperative efforts for mandatory training with Korean Patent Attorneys Association and strengthen and stabilize the homepage and increase usage through more frequent and regular updates.

To bring these objectives to fruition, the executive committee organized annual workshops for "strengthening the competitive ability for international business" for young patent attorneys so that the younger generation of patent attorneys can see the potential for international business opportunities through APAA and to encourage more of them to join as members. We received amazingly positive responses from these workshops.

We also created programs to support intellectual property rights in developing countries through which we dispatched our members abroad, such as Myanmar and Malaysia, and helped to bring educational programs that focused on improving intellectual property rights system and recent major developments in this area.

Previously, Korea-Japan joint meetings were held mostly with Patent Sub-Committee in mind. We enlarged the scope of these joint meetings by implementing regularly scheduled Korea-Japan joint events for Trademark Sub-Committee and Design Sub-Committee as well, and as a result, more members of all experiences can now participate in international activities. Further, we enjoyed great success at the Osaka Seminar and Tokyo Seminar which dealt with the topic of Samsung vs Apple cases with more than 300 participants attending both events.

Further, our Chapter was represented by more than 140 members at the General Meeting and Council Meeting in Chiang Mai in 2012, the Council Meeting in Hanoi in 2013 and the Council Meeting in Penang in 2014. We also had an average of 110 members for the Korean Night events that sought to promote mutual relationships among members.

At the Chiang Mai General Meeting in 2012, where election for the presidency was held for the first time in APAA's history, we were able to bring a certain country's bureaucratic dominance in APAA to an end by serving as an effective casting vote in the election. At this General Meeting in Chiang Mai, I proposed formation of a meeting of the presidents from each Chapter which was adopted. When the meeting of the presidents at the Penang Council Meeting was mired in a stalemate, I served as its temporary coordinator and helped to restore the meetings. These activities helped to build the right foundation for our Chapter to serve the role of an opinion leader at the APAA International.

I can say with confidence that we contributed substantially to enhancing the Korean Chapter's standing and improving the rights and interests of our members by actively engaging in international events through Committees and by strengthening our Chapter's leadership at the APAA International through participation of our co-chairs and delegates from five committees, which included one Adhoc Committee and four Standing Committees. We were also successful in completing the research service program on the issue of official fees for patent attorneys which became one of the most critical issues in terms of ensuring the rights and interests of patent attorneys.

It was very important for me to increase opportunities to interact with the senior members of the patent law community for the Korean Chapter as well as for Korean Patent Attorneys Association who have worked to build the patent attorneys bar into the status that it enjoys now. In this regard, I revitalized the past presidents group to also take advantage of the wealth of knowledge and information they possess.

We received great responses from the young patent attorneys by inviting the senior patent attorneys to the young patent attorneys' workshop to speak on their experiences and business know-how. Our ability to achieve the stated objectives was made possible because of the invaluable advice and generous support and love from our senior patent attorneys. I express my deep gratitude and appreciation to all of the past presidents as well as to each member.

Our executive committee sincerely believes that we were able to achieve most of the programs envisioned through the ten objectives. On the other hand, one program that we were not able to enjoy a positive result, even though we exerted much effort, was in increasing membership. While we were able to achieve internal stability, we were not able to increase membership. In fact, our total membership dropped a little due to our bold decision to revoke the membership of members who failed to pay their fees for an extended period. I must apologize for this situation, and I sincerely hope that the newly-elected President and the new executive committee can achieve better results towards this end.

I believe that achieving our ten objectives would have been impossible without the passion and sacrifices of each member of our executive committee who displayed tremendous wisdom and overflowing energy. I take this opportunity to thank each and every member of the executive committee from the bottom of my heart.

Once again, I want to thank all the members and the members of the executive committee who have provided unsparing support and encouragement for me to carry on my role and to serve as the President. Dear honorable members, I pray for your continued health and happiness as you continue your involvement with Asia Patent Lawyers community and for your continued success in your business.

February 27, 2015
Respectfully yours,

Ho Hyun Nahm, 11th President of the Korean Chapter of the Asia Patent Attorneys Association

I am grateful for the active cooperation I received from all of the members during my tenure as the President of the Korean Chapter of the Asia Patent

Attorneys Association. In many cases, the presidency is an honorary position. There is generally no compensation. However, there is unfortunately always a group of people who, instead of helping those who volunteer their precious time and energy as President or member of the executive committee, simply criticize and try to rattle the saber.

Constructive criticisms act as effective medicine for progress. But there are those who simply want to disparage. Without offering any alternatives. It is important to have a creative alternative and to be persuasive in communicating it. Whether a small family unit or at work, let's become leaders as a creative minority.

VIRTUAL AUGMENTED REALITY OF POKEMON GO

The entire country is going berserk with people everywhere trying to catch Pokemon Go characters. Of course, the characters do not actually exist in any physical form anywhere. It's just an imaginary thing that appears real.

Be that as it may, this is a character that appears everywhere, including next to my desk, my kitchen at home, at a park where I walk or by the roadside. It's known as augmented reality (AR), a technology which combines the imaginary space with the actual person's location using GPS technology and camera.

Although called augmented reality, it doesn't actually take place in the real world. It merely creates the illusion of reality, and it only takes place in the imaginary world.

I never had a special interest in computer games, as I always thought that they were not very productive. However, I can imagine that there is nothing more amazing and fun for those people who enjoy the computer games.

Domain name refers to the doorplate and Internet address of the virtual world, the very space on which the games are downloaded and where online shopping mall also known as the Internet Marketplace, personal homepage and company's website actual operates. The special characteristic of this Internet address lies in its uniqueness - it is the only one in the whole world.

It is possible for identical trademarks that are used on identical designated goods to exist in each country, independent of one another. However, Internet addresses don't work that way. Now, it is common for people to locate their desired cyberspace by conducting a search of key words through a portal site. But when the Internet address is easy to remember and is identical to the actual name, people can enter the site by directly typing in the address. As such, it is critical, especially for a company, to acquire an address for its virtual space that is the same as the name for the company or product.

Unlike trademarks, Internet address does not require distinctiveness. There are numerous cases where someone made a lot of money by registering a popular common or generic name as an Internet address. By spending less than hundred dollars for the registration fee, a huge sum of money could be had.

In a way, selling an Internet address with a generic name can be likened to the legendary fraudster Seondal Kim who sold water of the Great Taedong River to unsuspecting people. But the real problem lies in cybersquatters, those who first acquire the Internet address registration for a name that is identical or similar to another company's well-known tradename or trademark and then demand payment from that company in return for transfer of that registration.

A cybersquatter is a person who first acquires an Internet domain registration in the form of a well-known trademark, product or company name, and then seeks to sell the same registration, with a hefty premium, back to the original owner of the trademark or company who needs it to conduct business. Not only do they make it impossible for companies who want to provide Internet services to their customers, but this naturally leads to the abuse of extracting substantial payment from those companies. The recent public discussion in this area has been to legally restrict such behavior.

To this extent, while Pope Francis exhibited his skills in IT by utilizing a Twitter account in 2013, it was reported that even the Vatican failed to acquire the domain name for the Pope right after his election.

Further, there are those who use a name similar to an existing Internet domain address to lure potential customers or entice users to click on to porn sites or counterfeit product sites. The consequential damages from such cybersquatting activities that use such advertising sites as baits do not appear to be declining.

In response to the prevalence of these incidents, there are now efficient, fair and inexpensive procedures in place that enable companies and individuals with valid rights to cancel or recover the domain name registrations that had been previously occupied by cybersquatters.

INTERNET DOMAIN ADDRESS DISPUTES - EFFICIENT, FAIR AND INEXPENSIVE RESOLUTION

In an Internet domain address, there are generic top level domains (gTLDs), which end in .com, .net, .org, .samsung and .hyundai, and country code top level domains (ccTLDs) such as .kr, .jp, .us, and .uk which indicate Korea, Japan, U.S. and U.K. respectively.

The institution that is responsible for coordinating the maintenance and procedure for gTLDs is The Internet Corporation for Assigned Names and Numbers (ICANN), who has adopted Uniform Domain Name Dispute Resolution Policy (UDRP). UDRP requires, as a condition to registration, the domain name applicant to adhere to UDRP procedures on dispute resolution in the event there is an issue with a third party in connection with the registered domain name.

Relief comes only in two forms - one is "cancellation" and the other is "transfer" of the domain name registration. Once a decision is rendered, it is binding regardless of whether either party is satisfied or not. Unless a party files a complaint before a court having jurisdiction over the case within a given time period, the decision can be readily enforced without regard to territorial borders.

Because a decision is generally issued within 2-3 months from the date of filing, it is so much more efficient and inexpensive when compared with court procedures. The proceeding is quite fair as the Administrative Panelist, selected from all over the world, possesses special expertise and conducts the examination in a fair manner. This process also provides recourse to the courts.

ICANN, the responsible institution for assigning Internet addresses, has approved five institutions as dispute resolution centers, including World Intellectual Property Organization (WIPO) which is one of the UN-affiliated organizations, National Arbitration Forum (NAF), Asia Doman Name Dispute Resolution Centre (ADNDRC), The Czech Arbitration Court (CAC) and Arab Center for Domain Name Dispute Resolution (ACDR). More than 90% of the cases are handled by WIPO and NAF.

In the case of the disputes involving country code top level domains (ccTLDs) such as .kr, .jp, .us, and .uk, which indicate Korea, Japan, U.S. and U.K. respectively, most countries have in place procedures similar to UDRP to handle them. In Korea, "Domain Name Dispute Resolution Committee" was installed in 2000 to handle these matters, and currently, the Korea Internet address Dispute Resolution Committee was set up as the legal institution under the "Act relating to Internet Address Resources" and governs the function of domain name dispute resolution involving .kr.

The procedure is quite similar to that of UDRP. Less than 10% of the cases actually end up in the courts as a result of a party refusing to accept the decision made by the members of our Committee. Even among those cases that are reviewed by the courts, less than 1% actually reach a result different from that reached by the members of our Committee. The impact of our Council's decisions is great when compared with the tremendous time and expense incurred in litigating the case before the court, and as such, it serves as an effective alternative. I believe that this approach to dispute resolution can apply effectively to not just Internet address disputes but also other areas as well, and in this regard, I urge the legal community to take a serious interest in how this can be applied.

REACHING 500 DECISIONS ON DOMAIN NAME DISPUTE CASES

I am currently registered as a Panelist (Arbitrator) on WIPO, NAF, ADNDRC and CAC. Once a specific case is assigned, a Panelist renders a decision on a case, similar to that issued by a judge. In this process, the Panelist writes a decision more or less 10 pages which provides in detail the reasons for the decision. The language used in this process is basically determined by the specific language that is used in the registration agreement.

In looking back, I had already issued decisions on 500 cases. Of them, 80% of the decisions were written in English, and 20% in Korean and Japanese. Considering that each decision is about 10 pages, the total pages covering all the decisions I wrote add up to about 5,000 pages using A4 paper. In case this was prepared in individual books, it would comprise a grand series of 50 books.

Most of the decisions I wrote can be searched using my last name, Nahm, on each of the home pages decision search site at WIPO (www.wipo.org), NAF (www.adrforum.com), ADNDRC (www.adndrc.org) and CAC (https://udrp.adr.eu).

Where there is no conflict of interest, I have represented my clients in trying to resolve a dispute on their behalf. It was in one of these cases where I helped to establish one of the leading trademark cases while representing Hyundai Motor Company and its chairman, Mong-Koo Chung where I prevailed in getting the chairman's name, "Mong-Koo Chung", to be recognized as a common-law trademark.

Indeed, I have participated with passion in the discussion of issues relating to Internet address dispute resolution as a Panelist (arbitrator) of WIPO, NAF, ADNDRC and CAC, and also as a member serving a total of 16 years starting as the founding member of Korea's Domain Name Dispute Resolution Committee and as a member of its successor group, Internet Address Dispute Resolution Committee (governmental organization). For the last three years, I served as the chairman of the latter group to preside over its general meetings and workshops, international seminars, executive committee meetings and the publication of the white paper on these disputes.

On numerous occasions, I wrote papers in this area, presented scholarly paper, gave lectures and wrote the Korean Chapter of "Domain Name Handbook" published by Oxford University Press. I am filled with joy to have contributed to the wide acceptance of the new method of dispute resolution that is different in nature from a simple mediation or arbitration.

THE ROAD TO CRUSHING PATENT TROLLS IN THE PATENT WAR

The following summarizes the discussions I had while appearing in the KBS 1 radio show called "Intuitive Success, This Is Banghee Kim." [© KBS, Feeling of Success: Kim Bang Hee]

-"Intuitive Success" http://www.kbs.co.kr/radio/1radio/plus/talk/job.html

-Host: Banghee Kim, Chief Researcher, Life Economics

▲ Banghee Kim: There are largely two situations where most people take interest in the patent attorney profession. One is when the media reports, more or less annually, that the patent attorneys earn the highest income. Also, our society takes much interest when patent attorneys are featured prominently in patent wars that involve our companies against foreign companies or patent trolls. With this type of focus and attention, this profession has become popular among the younger generations. A lot of people are preparing to enter this profession.

Some say, however, that a closer look reveals a lot of misunderstanding and bias. In today's "secrets to success" hour, I will be speaking with a leading patent attorney in Korea to correct any misunderstanding and to confirm the truth in connection with the patent attorney profession as well as how to be ready for the patent wars likely to come in the future.

Please welcome patent attorney, Ho Hyun Nahm, who is the author of "Change Your Life with Ideas."

◖ Banghee Kim: We hear a lot about the patent attorney profession, but not too many people know accurately what this profession does. What do you do?

🅐 Ho Hyun Nahm: It no longer is the case now, but about 30 years ago when I took the patent attorney examination, patent attorney was relatively unknown. Some believed that patent attorneys were accountants or chicken sexers. Some called it the "star director" given its unique pronunciation.

But actually, patent attorneys engage in wide-ranging activities. We represent clients in acquiring intellectual property rights or exclusive rights to intellectual property, including patents relating to all technical areas or Internet business methods, utility models, product designs and trademarks, service marks relating to restaurants and entertainment business and domain names. We also help resolve disputes involving intellectual property, including representing clients in invalidation actions, scope confirmation trials or cancellation of decision before the Korean Intellectual Property Tribunal, the Patent Court and the Supreme Court. We are also engaged in appraisal and analysis of rights for use in infringement issues, corporation management consulting services involving intellectual property, protection of trade secrets and execution of license agreements.

🅒 Banghee Kim: It's not as often now, but the patent attorney profession was often reported as earning the highest income. Is that true?

🅐 Ho Hyun Nahm: Until a few years ago, patent attorney profession was identified by the National Tax Office as having the highest income among all professions. But I understand that there are now patent attorneys who struggle financially because of drastic and consistent rise in the number of patent attorneys and the relative decline in the filing of patents in the last few years. The time where a handful of patent attorneys dominated this industry is long gone, and I believe that we have entered a merit-based, competitive period.

🅒 Banghee Kim: We just thought that patent attorneys would continue to do well since the disputes involving patents and trademarks continue to grow between not only companies but also individuals. I guess this is not the case?

🅐 Ho Hyun Nahm: It may have been true so far. It is not an exaggeration to say that intellectual property such as patents, designs, trademarks and tradenames will be one of the most critical and important elements to a successful business management, whether the business involves a conglomerate, small-sized enterprise or sole proprietorship. Acquiring competitive advantage through intellectual property is the secret to the survival and success of a business, and as such, I think that the patent attorney profession that deals with intellectual property work will continue to remain a promising occupation.

However, the problem lies in the imbalance of supply and demand in light of the recent drastic increase in the number of patent attorneys relative to the demands for their work.

Q Banghee Kim: You are well known for working on many of the landmark cases in patent disputes. What are the elements to success as a patent attorney?

A Ho Hyun Nahm: I'm not sure if landmark is the appropriate description, but I take special pride in having successfully argued cases that many assumed to have a very low chance of success in light of the prevailing legal principles or applicable case law.

The key to success as a patent attorney, I believe, is continuing to update new information and knowledge.

I make it a daily routine to engage in writing about educating and enlightening the general public on intellectual property issues, actively participate and give presentations in numerous domestic and international seminars and enthusiastically read new decisions and writings on these issues. I especially want to point out the importance of possessing the ability to have a positive perspective from the viewpoint of the client, creative mindset that can overturn conventional wisdom and current trend, persistence to never give up, and lastly, diligence and sincerity.

Q Banghee Kim: For you personally, which case involving an intellectual property dispute do you find most memorable and meaningful to the society?

A Ho Hyun Nahm: There are a number of cases in which I take much pride and satisfaction. I will talk about one of them. There was a company in the U.S. that acquired a domain name registration in the name of the chairman of a Korean conglomerate and was operating a website that was highly critical of the Korean company.

As the counsel for the chairman of this Korean conglomerate, I filed a complaint for transfer of the relevant domain name registrations with WIPO, which is a UN affiliated organization. One of the elements that we needed to prove to prevail in this case was that the disputed domain name was identical or substantially similar to the applicant's trademark. This was a problem because the name of the chairman of the Korean conglomerate had never been registered as a trademark in Korea or anywhere else. In most cases, the name of the chairman of a conglomerate is not even considered a trademark.

I decided to focus on the argument that a trademark serves the function of identifying the source of its goods. I prepared and presented voluminous evidence to show that the name of this chairman was sufficient to evoke precisely the very industry in that field. In so doing, I argued and proved that the name of this chairman was in fact a common law trademark.

The WIPO Panelist accepted my arguments and ruled in favor of my client, and as a result, we acquired the domain name registrations. I believe that this decision has a real significance socially as well.

Q Banghee Kim: We hear often about patent trolls who purchase patents from companies and then use those patents to engage in indiscriminate patent lawsuits against multinational companies. Some say that these lawsuits especially target Korean companies. Is that true?

A Ho Hyun Nahm: Patent trolls are patent specialty management companies who do not engage in production or manufacturing of actual products, but who acquire certain ideas or patented technologies from universities, research centers, individuals or company and sue other company who are infringing on such patents. They make their profit from patent lawsuits and settlements on these infringement actions.

One of the leading patent troll is called Intellectual Ventures. It is a company created with $5 billion funded by Microsoft, Intel, Sony, Nokia, Apple, Google and eBay, with 650 employees and 30,000 patents. Relevant data shows that as of April 2010, there are about 300 patent trolls operating throughout the world.

It has been reported that Samsung Electronics and LG Electronics have been sued by these patent trolls and were forced to pay hundreds of millions of dollars through patent infringement lawsuits or settlements.

What is even more shocking is that these foreign patent trolls have opened their branch offices in Korea and are involved in purchasing patents from our universities as well as our conglomerates, which in turn are used to attack Korean companies. It can be said that we are being attacked with our own developed technologies.

I believe that our private companies need to start recognizing the enormous value in the successful results obtained from university research programs. I also believe that it is necessary for our government and companies to jointly establish a fund to form our own Korean patent trolls to prevent the outflow of our local technology. We also need to respond to the attacks of these patent trolls by utilizing the legal principles of "abuse of rights" and "no damage accrues to a company not engaged in business" that are recognized under the current laws. Towards this end, I believe the government needs to basically step up its efforts to initiate international cooperation to find a global legislative solution to this serious issue.

Banghee Kim: At one time, Korean companies paid a big price for not being prepared and not fully understanding the concept of intellectual property. What's the situation now?

Ho Hyun Nahm: That has declined quite a bit compared to the past. But there are still a plenty of situations where a company simply losses its competitive advantage because of its inability to respond properly to a competitor's piracy or copying, or in some cases, is forced to close its business after a patent infringement lawsuit is filed against them.

Of course, there are cases where a Korean export company is forced to discontinue its exports to its destination country because it failed to properly register its trademark in that country or otherwise sustains tremendous losses from an infringement lawsuit.

Intellectual property protection is a necessity and not just an option. In the old days, countries sought to expand their territories through wars using weapons. In the current intellectual information society, I am confident that any individual, company or even a nation can expand their territory through acquisition of intellectual property rights.

Q Banghee Kim: There are a lot of young people who blindly seek to become a patent attorney based only on what they hear from the media. With this market becoming somewhat polarized, it would appear that those who have the temperament and is well suited to this profession should be encouraged to pursue it. What advice do you have for young people who aspire to become a patent attorney?

A Ho Hyun Nahm: Patent attorney is an attractive occupation because the work of a patent attorney entails becoming a partner to the creation of new value. I still enjoy working as a patent attorney and find much satisfaction. But the time when a patent attorney is assured of high earnings has passed. It may even be difficult to make ends meet unless you are truly a competent patent attorney.

You can become a successful patent attorney if you truly like the work and train yourself legally as well as technically, and in addition, possess the requisite language skills likely to be required given the international nature of a patent attorney's work and are prepared to tirelessly keep up with updated information and knowledge. I certainly hope that more and more young people can have a dream and challenge to become a patent attorney.

EDISON, THE KING OF INVENTION, AND PENNILESS

-Win without fighting. Never litigate-

After years of long and tedious litigation, the Pittsburgh Circuit Court declared Thomas Edison as the prevailing party. Westinghouse promptly filed an appeal, but Edison ultimately won, as he predicted. But the money he had to pay for legal fees in this litigation amounted to millions of dollars.

The day that he received a decision in his favor after enduring such bitter struggle, Edison started calculating the remaining term of his patent right. He quickly discovered that he just had two years remaining in the patent term for his incandescent light bulb patent. He was literally penniless when he walked out of his company after giving up his ownership to a third party.

There may be no other people in the world like Koreans when it comes to suing others. Based on data, the rate of litigation per person is the highest in Korea. If so, why do people want to litigate? Who actually stands to gain from this propensity to easily get enraged and file a lawsuit with the court?

It's often said that three years of litigation lead to ruins. But most cases take more than three years. Some people actually become extremely ill from the stress and mental pressure. The time dedicated to the lawsuit, however, prevents a person from engaging in productive work. It is entirely possible that a family or a company can be wrecked while involved in a lawsuit.

I was playing golf and talking with a chairman of a medium-sized company and who is someone I respect much and who also went to my school

20 years before me. He was lamenting, knowing that I was a patent attorney specializing in patents.

"I am currently in a patent infringement lawsuit because some company is infringing on my amazing patent."

He said that he retained a major law firm in Korea and that he himself was so personally involved in collecting evidence and helping to prepare briefs that he even had serious run-ins with the managing partner of that firm during this process. Indeed, this has become a major lawsuit. He desperately wanted me to take a serious interest in it. There was a bucketful of USB memory sticks he gave me that contained the records in this case.

"How do you see this case?"

He asked for my opinion.

LAWYERS ARE ALL IN HELL

"Let me ask you, chairman. There are two parties fighting fiercely over a cow. One has his grip on the horn, while the other has the tail, and both are putting out all their strengths to prevail. What do you think the lawyer is doing in between while the two parties are fighting?"

I threw an off-the-wall question at him after listening to him intently.

"Well, what would the lawyer be doing?"

"He would be working hard to represent his client in court."

"No, chairman. The lawyer would be milking the cow."

"Wow, hard to believe!"

He then seemed to have an aha moment.

In the U.S., a concerted effort is made to settle the case prior to litigation. To the extent practicable, they go through mediation, and if settlement is not reached, then lawsuit gets filed. Even litigation is not simply used as a way to fight all the way to the end to obtain a judgement. In the course of a lawsuit, both parties' main arguments are more or less laid out. It becomes pretty clear who has stronger arguments.

"There is definitely a clear advantage in this process. Ultimately, litigation is used more as a negotiating tool. Most litigations end in settlements."

He understood what I was trying to say, and he immediately sought someone who can act as a go-between for the litigating parties. Then, the case was settled, he received a substantial settlement money and he withdrew his infringement lawsuit.

"You don't know how free my mind and body feel after withdrawing the patent lawsuit. I'm also happy with the settlement terms. Otherwise, I would still be stressing over it, wasting my precious time and paying huge legal fees."

Needless to say, the smile on that chairman's face when I next saw him made me very happy.

A legal dispute arose between heaven and hell. The wall that separated heaven and hell came crumbling down. The fierce dispute was over who is responsible for the repair. There was an end to this. Who won? Hell… Why?

Because there are no lawyers in heaven, and thus, heaven could not hire a lawyer. Lawyers were all in hell, and given its firepower, hell won. Of course, this is a joke that makes fun of unscrupulous lawyers. But it's also true that the longer a lawsuit takes, the more it fills the lawyer's pocket.

My grandkids, you must first negotiate before fighting. Even if you have to find someone to serve as a bridge, make the effort to mediate. If you have no choice but to litigate, remember that your objective is to use it as a negotiating tool and reach resolution.

You should know that this process requires the counsel of a lawyer or patent attorney. You can sustain substantial damages by meeting the other party alone if you try to save money without consulting a lawyer or patent attorney beforehand. You shouldn't be afraid to spend money on the fees of a lawyer or a patent attorney. Otherwise, you may need a spade when a hoe would have been enough. Remember, you will win every battle if you know yourself and your enemy. By precisely understanding the crux of the issue, anyone can all prevail without fighting.

FINALLY A MILLION MILER

-007 Plan at Charles de Gaulle Airport
and John F. Kennedy Airport-

One day, I received a plaque from someone out of the blue. I wasn't expecting one, so I unwrapped the package with some curiosity and suspicion.

"We celebrate your admission to membership on our Korean Air Million Miler Club, with your qualifying flight on KE 906 on June 23, 2012. Flight from Frankfurt to Incheon on Korean Air."

This message was written on a nice-looking crystal trophy. It had been 24 years since my first maiden overseas and my first business trip to Phoenix, Arizona in 1988. The one million mileage represents the actual miles flown on Korean Air and its partner airlines.

It's not that I flew only on Korean Air; I needed to travel to every nook and cranny to catch fish in the deepest waters. Asiana, Air France, American Air, British Air, Air Canada, Japan Airlines, Cathay Pacific, Air China, and Lufthansa, to name a few that I can recall.

But I used Korean Air the most because I had a special affinity and care for Korean Air for two reasons.

One, Korean Air is my previous job. Korean Air was my previous employer, after I passed its open competitive employment examination and received valuable experience and memories working at its legal department, and as such, I have always preferred flying Korean Air. Two, of all the many airlines I have been on, Korean Air is actually in a world class by itself as an airline.

Above anything else, it is the cleanest. Delay in baggage arrivals or other minor issues and inconveniences are almost nonexistent. Well-arranged and fresh in-flight meals work quite well for my taste. Flight attendants are courteous, elegant and kind. The ramen soup they prepare is especially tasty. Bibimbap is uniquely good. I should mention that I was the one that recommended "jook" (rice porridge) as an in-flight menu item, and I take pleasure in watching many passengers enjoy this food for breakfast. On the other hand, its airfare is probably the most expensive. But the flights are always full.

I remember when I was in a new employee training program at Korean Air. There was a special lecture given by Mr. Joong Hoon Cho, the chairman of the Hanjin Group, to which Korean Air belonged. Chairman Cho gave a spirited lecture about living with passion.

"In my eyes, money is floating all over. I'm not sure why people don't stop to think about grabbing it when all you need to do is reach out and grab it."

This was from Chairman Cho, who made a fortune after signing a contract to transport supplies for the U.S. military during the Vietnam War.

"During the Vietnam War, the drivers of the trucks with military cargoes simply did not want to work with bullets flying all around and the sound of gunfires everywhere."

Only when Chairman Cho himself took the lead and his vice president took the tail of the truck convoy did everyone else start to move. Even to the leaders of the conglomerates who see money floating all around, nothing is achieved for free. The end result is a reflection of the best effort, as if your life depended on it.

Having assumed that all conglomerates made their wealth through cozy relationships with government and corruption, I was ashamed. Chairman Cho is a representative figure of a creative minority who has become a global leader in the transport industry. After having made his fortune from the transport business in Vietnam War, he was called in by President Chung Hee Park.

He was told to take over Korean Air, which was a debt-ridden, government-owned enterprise at the time. The story has it that Chairman Cho refused the proposal three times because it was obvious to anybody that it would have been akin to pouring water into a bottomless pit.

But President Park strongly persisted in recommending the takeover. Although the takeover took place reluctantly, Korean Air has now been transformed into one of the top three airlines in the world. Creative best efforts from gifted businessmen, such as Hyundai Chairman Joo-Young Chung, Samsung Chairman Byung Chul Lee and Hanjin Chairman Joong Hoon Cho have laid the foundation for making Korea into the success story that she is now.

Yes. Even at this moment, your good luck is floating around you. Be courageous, push out and get up. Reach out and grab your good luck. Take a look at your family, people and all matters around you with a new perspective and new mindset. You will begin to see a new world.

Having flown so many times around the world, enough to become a million miler, I have had my share of scheduling mix-ups from time to time. One time, it happened when I was working at Central International Patent and Law Firm. Traveling with office colleagues, we finished our business trip to Europe and were going to the Paris Charles de Gaulle Airport to catch a flight to New York. In those days, they cancelled your reservations if you didn't reconfirm.

Of course, I had reconfirmed our reservations. But what is this? They said there was no seat on the flight. The airline had overbooked - Trans World Airlines. The real problem was that my flight was the last flight to New York on that Sunday.

We had a meeting scheduled for 10 am the following Monday morning with the chief intellectual property officer of a multinational client located in New Jersey, which is near New York, along with 10 other officers, including the representative of this client's subsidiary who was coming to the meeting from a remote location. We would not be able to get to this meeting on time if we didn't get on this flight. Sky seemed to be falling. The check-in counter for this flight was a total chaos :

"I am an obstetrician. I must go and deliver a baby."

"I am a university professor. I can't miss a lecture."

"I need to be at my father's deathbed."

Everybody clamored for a seat on the flight. It was understandable since the next day was a Monday. Surely, the worker at the check-in desk wouldn't bat an eye over "an important meeting with a client" excuse. I first sent a fax to the New Jersey client notifying them of my situation,

"I'm sorry. We may not be able to make it to the meeting on time."

Because of the importance of this meeting, it was obvious that we would lose much credibility if we couldn't get to the meeting on time, regardless of the reason. Moreover, we could not miss this meeting because the issues to be discussed there were urgent and critical. The airline takes responsibility for overbooking, and they issue a voucher for an overnight stay at a hotel. Pretty ridiculous.

My desperate desire to keep the promise with the client compelled me to think and rethink about any alternative approaches. Is there any way I can fly out to New York? As someone who worked for an airline, I started asking questions all over the airport.

"What's the use of asking for something that is physically impossible?"

My colleagues scoffed at me. But the door only opens when you knock. There was a way to get to the 10 am meeting at the client's office in New Jersey even after spending the Sunday night in Paris.

It was the Concorde, the supersonic aircraft made jointly by U.K. and France. It would leave at 8 am from Paris and arrive at New York's John F. Kennedy Airport by 8 am local time, after which a helicopter can take us to Manhattan from the John F. Kennedy Airport. I figured that taking a taxi from Manhattan should give us sufficient time to get to the client's office in New Jersey by 9:30 am. The only drawback was that only first class seats were in operation and the airfare was outrageously expensive.

On a regular flight, Paris to New York flight generally takes eight hours. On the Concorde, it takes four hours from Paris to New York, and considering the time difference, four more hours would be saved. After arrival in New York, the custom clearance process was supersonic fast, thanks to the escort. We were finally on the helicopter.

It was obvious that regular traffic on a Monday morning would have been super slow. But we took the supersonic plane to John F. Kennedy Airport and then the helicopter to Manhattan. I felt like the superspy James Bond in the 007 movie series. From Manhattan, we took a taxi to the client company.

After all this, the confident taxi driver who said he knew exactly where to go got lost and kept driving aimlessly. When we got to the client's office, it was 10:15 am, 15 minutes later than the scheduled meeting time. The ten or so executive officers of the client company who were waiting for us gave us a loud standing ovation. That was because I had been sending them faxes informing them of the details of our trip.

The meeting went well. It was obvious that we earned more credibility and trust from our client company as a result. Before I became a million miler, I was fortunate enough to ride in a variety of planes, including the 7-person light aircraft over my Grand Canyon trip, the helicopter ride over Manhattan and the supersonic Concorde.

The Concorde is no longer in operation due to technical issues, which means that no one can ride it even if they wanted to. This was an experience which proved to me that you can always find a way even against impossible odds if you believe in it and you make the effort. This is indeed a sweet memory for me every time I think about it.

EAGLE SOARING HIGH IN THE SKY

The entire country is in brouhaha over the Law on the Prevention of Illicit Solicitation and Bribery, also known as Young Ran Kim Law.

"It is unconstitutional to subject journalists and staff member of private schools to this Law."

"Parliamentary members are in fact not subject to the Law's application."

"The real victims are the florists, livestock farmers, farmers and restaurant owners who produce or deal in such items as flowers, meat and fruits that are commonly used as gifts or where people are wined and dined. Once this law takes effect, their business will suffer significantly."

Many pros and cons abound. I would think that there will be people negatively impacted by its implementation. But we should not abandon the road that we must travel because of such concerns.

When engaged in work, situations arise where it becomes necessary to exchange mutual benefits with a client or someone related to the work for a better working relationship, not necessarily to just ask for a favor. The nature of the patent attorney profession is such that if the patent attorney is the fish, clients are the water, and a fish cannot live out of the water. We need to ensure that our relationship with the client remains uninterrupted. But I just hate going out drinking. I don't enjoy alcohol, and I dislike the traditional entertaining, wining and dining culture even more.

As a no-choice alternative, I decided to start golf. The fact that I can enjoy a sports activity with someone for five or so hours and engage in dialogue with them in the process was quite appealing. But starting golf in my early 50's wasn't going to help to hit the ball better. As soon as I started golf, a group of patent attorneys was planning a golf trip to China. My wife, at my urging, also started golf. This was a group for married couples.

"If you bet while playing golf, you'll get riled up, and this will make you learn even faster and practice harder."

At a time when I wasn't even familiar with the word "strokes,"

an older and senior patent attorney suggested that we bet while playing golf. Since I was a worse player than him, he gave me some money in advance as a handicap. My ball was rolling more than flying in the air, and my score was too much to even keep counting. The money I received as handicap was already gone early. I was really riled up.

"I'm going to quit golf as of today."

With this thought in mind, I was hoping that the miserable round would soon be over. I was so frustrated that day, I have not played "strokes" game since.

We have a group made up of friends who are patent attorneys called IPGA. IP represents the first letters in the word, intellectual property, and GA for golf association. And that's just not in name only. Some of the members are practically professionals. We have monthly outings, and at the end of each year, we have a championship tournament to award the best player.

This took place on November 19, 2008 at New Seoul Country Club, North Course. Extra strokes were given to beginner players based on their previous scores, with a maximum number of strokes set. Usually, we played in the afternoons, but that day, we decided to play in the morning. The weather was so cold that the greens were practically frozen.

Even the best players who usually reach the greens-in-regulation (reaching the green in two strokes less than the par score) were losing shots left and right because the balls would simply bounce off the frozen greens. Since I was not good enough to reach the greens-in-regulation, I just tried to get close and then roll the ball unto the greens. My strategy worked that day, and my shots felt good. People in my group were enjoying the outing and they were very generous in giving conceded putts (Concede means an acknowledgement by other players in your group that you are assumed to have made your next putt without the need to actually play the next putt). While our group's internal rules dictate that concedes may only be given if the remaining putt is within a certain distance, whether to concede was a decision that rested squarely on your playing partners.

For the first time in a while, I scored in the 80s. Even better, I was declared the champion! I was the 2008 champion of champions. I wasn't sure if it was real or just a dream? I couldn't believe that I won the year-end championship. I was probably happier than a professional winning his or her first PGA or LPGA win. I still proudly display the championship trophy bearing the golf ball made of pure gold on my desk.

Then, it finally happened on January 24, 2010 at Kihung Country Club, North Course, Hole #6. On a Par 5 hole, if you put the ball in the hole in five strokes, that is a par and is considered a good score for an amateur. If you put the ball in the hole in four strokes, that is a birdie and a very good score. If you only take three strokes to put the ball in the hole, then it is called an eagle - named after the King of the birds. All amateurs dream of getting an eagle, as it is considered to be a more difficult and valuable than a hole-in-one.

Everybody shouted "nice shot" when I hit my third shot from about 110 meters away. I thought that the ball landed on the green. I couldn't be sure where the ball ended up because the green was elevated from where I just hit the ball. But when I got on the green, I didn't see my ball.

"I know I hit it pretty well..."

I was muttering to myself, as I couldn't even find my ball even outside of the green.

"Look in the hole!"

The caddy yelled. No way. There was my ball, clearly bearing with my marks, and smiling and welcoming me!

"Wow, it's an eagle! It's an eagle!"

My partners screamed out in unison. Among this group was the older and senior patent attorney who asked to play for money for strokes when I was just a fledgling beginner.

"No way, is this true?"

Looking as if he couldn't believe it, the older patent attorney came up and then just shook his head after seeing that it really was my ball. They say that the odds of getting an eagle are more difficult than the 12,000 to 1 odds for a hole-in-one. My partners made a commemorative eagle trophy with the same ball and presented it to me. In response, I held a party for the married couples. What started out as a way to improve communications and relations with clients have turned into a real hobby. Although I'm still not very good, I won a trophy and even scored an eagle.

Golf even helped me get closer to my wife. Since we both enjoyed golf, we would practice together, play golf together, watch television programs together, and found common topics to discuss. I was delighted to spend so much more time with my beloved wife. The more I think about it, I think that the decision to start golf was a very good one. It also helps in maintaining relationships with a client every now and then. However, my interest in golf has since waned quite a bit after losing my partner with whom I shared so much joy.

My beloved wife, Jungsook Julie, was my life and the very purpose of my existence. My efforts in pursuing success, writing books, making good earnings, working to play better golf were all things that I did to earn brownie points for, and to look good to, my wife who was my life partner. Losing that partner rendered all of the things I strived for somewhat meaningless. It was my mother who gave me life and raised me well, and it was my wife who made me who I am today. I miss her. I miss her more. I miss her with all my heart.

My wife was involved in many meaningful activities and then suddenly left to be with God. I have now set new life goals for myself so that I can help achieve the mission that she wasn't able to complete. This has led to activities that prompted a children's hospital to display a picture of my wife's beautiful golf swing in its lobby.

Having started golf in my late years, I read a lot of golf books. I also practiced diligently to prepare for the real games. While I try to put out my creative best efforts to work on a new swing, they simply laugh at me. They say that I get too low when swinging.

"You had such a wonderful and beautiful swing when you first started… now it's a mess."

My wife used to say the same thing. But I persist stubbornly. While others may laugh at me, I'm thinking that my latest swing form is the product of my unique and dazzling personality and my creative best effort.

JESUS NEVER GRADUATED
FROM ELEMENTARY SCHOOL

Andrew Johnson, the 17th President of the U.S., is a representative figure of those who demonstrated the power of positivity to the full extent. He lost his father when he was three years old, and he was so poor that he wasn't able to even set foot in a school. Ten years later at the age of thirteen, he began working in a tailor shop. Then four years later at the age of seventeen, he opened his own tailor shop and starting making a lot of money.

Andrew Johnson has the shortest resume among all presidents in terms of education. Lincoln's resume in this regard is a tiny bit longer than Johnson's. Johnson married the daughter of a shoe cobbler, and it was his wife who taught him how to read and write. He later began to take interest in culture and classics, and after amassing much knowledge in a variety of areas, he decided to become involved in politics. After serving as the governor of Tennessee, he served as a senator after which he took office as the vice president to President Lincoln, who is the 16th President. After Lincoln's assassination, he became the 17th President of the United States.

Andrew Johnson was known to be especially highly-skilled in debates with political enemies. When he was selected as the vice presidential candidate for the Democratic Party, the Republicans tried to make an issue out of his lack of educational background.

"Does it make sense that someone who did not even finish elementary school could be asked to lead a country? A man trained as a tailor shouldn't be seeking the presidency."

Andrew Johnson was confronted with harsh criticisms from the general public. As he always did, Johnson calmly responded. His words reversed the course:

"My fellow citizens, do you know whether Jesus finished elementary school? I have never heard that Jesus Christ even attended elementary school. Moreover, Jesus was a carpenter. Even though he never finished elementary school, Jesus is leading the entire mankind to salvation. The power that will lead this country is not the level of education. It's the positive will and the active support from the American people."

As the 17th President, Johnson instructed his Secretary of State William Seward to purchase the territory of Alaska (about 15 times larger than Korea and 7 times larger than the Korean peninsula) for $7,200,000 (equivalent to the current value of $123 million in 2016, about the same as the value of 70 expensive apartment condos in Kangnam). Even though many criticized his decision to purchase the "frozen land" of Alaska, it is historically well-known that he was able to complete this purchase by demonstrating the power of positive mind.

Hillary Clinton grew up in a middle-class family, with a mother who lived through extremely adverse conditions and father who was very stubborn. Her mother had been abandoned as a child, and she began work as a maid at the age of 14. Her father was a small business owner operating a small textile company. Her mother earned just $3 as a maid per week. Nonetheless, Hillary Clinton's role model is her mother. As someone who had a difficult childhood, Hillary's mother stimulated her daughter's sense of accomplishment and enthusiastically provided her support. Even now, Hillary Clinton speaks about how she will always remember the lessons her mother taught her.

"Everybody must become a champion."

This is the message left by her mother. Yes. To be a champion, we must guard against imitating without creativity and repeating the same like a parrot. The window of opportunity will open widely for the creative minority only when one desperately seeks to break the conventional norms and moves towards a creative life.

My grandkids, go and peacefully smash the wall of bias and the myopic decision-making process that you may have become so used to. People won't acknowledge you and will even ignore you if you act like you are the only wise and sensible one. You will be able to recognize obsolete and cave-like mindsets only by widening and enriching your vision. You need to transform creative ideas based on continuous inquiries into your own assets. This will allow you to learn the successful formula used by the creative minority.

My grandkids, don't boast about your educational background. Don't get too complacent just because you graduated from a prestigious university. On the other hand, don't be so fainthearted because you are not too highly educated or attended just a regional university. Don't dwell on your disadvantaged past.

Rely on the power of the Almighty God and never lose courage. Trust that dreams will come true. Create and protect your own everlasting value and work on cultivating and growing it. Cast your net on the deep side by using your creative perspective. You will ultimately be able to catch enough fish to tear up the net.

BOOK 2

BENEFICIARIES OF CREATIVE BEST EFFORT

*Leading or Landmark Cases Won by the Author through Creative Best Effort

THE BATTLE BETWEEN "SNOW PERFUME" AND "ICE SNOW"

- SNOW PERFUME vs. ICE SNOW -

"The other side filed an appeal seeking cancellation of the Original Decision with the Patent Court. We don't know what to do."

The person in charge of intellectual property at VOV Co., Ltd. came running. He came so fast that he was literally out of breath. After he gathered himself, we started discussing this matter step by step.

VOV Co., Ltd. had registered a trademark for "SNOW PERFUME" for cosmetic goods. Pacific Co., Ltd. took issue, arguing that VOV's trademark lacked distinctiveness. They had filed an action to invalidate the registration of "SNOW PERFUME" based on its similarity with their prior-registered mark "ICE SNOW." VOV somehow managed to defend this case before the Korean Intellectual Property Tribunal, but the other side filed an appeal with the Patent Court seeking to cancel the Original Decision.

"We have to win because the mark we are using now is extremely important to us."

The person in charge emphasized the need to win and asked me to represent them. His concern was justified as the issues in this case could not be taken lightly.

In the client's mark, SNOW PERFUME, the portion PERFUME is a generic term for perfumes which lacks distinctiveness. The word SNOW has the dictionary definition of "snow, pure white." When this term is used on its designated goods, "perfumes or lavender," it will be perceived by consumers as "white as snow," or "clean, pure", and as such, it constitutes a functional indication that directly indicates the characteristic (quality or efficacy) of its designated goods. In addition, there were already 24 marks containing "SNOW" or its Korean version that have been registered by others.

"SNOW lacks distinctiveness. Even if we were to prevail on this issue, it is highly likely that the marks themselves will be found similar in their entireties since the main element in our mark is identical to one of the elements of Pacific Co., Ltd.'s prior-registered mark, "ICE SNOW."

Having said that, I was agonizing over and over again to try to find a solution.

"Where there's a will, there's a way; let's meet the challenge."

Like a flash of light, a thought came to me. Yes, it was true that both SNOW and PERFUME lack the required distinctiveness as it pertains to cosmetic goods. But where non-distinctive elements, such as SNOW and PERFUME, combine to create a new special concept, the distinctiveness of the mark in its entirety should be recognized. If a mark is dissected into its elements for the purpose of determining similarity of marks, the concept that is newly created by combining those elements is rendered meaningless. As such, there must be some legal basis that allows for examination of the mark in its entirety.

"My client's mark, SNOW PERFUME, created a new concept 'SeolHyang' (a coined Korean word; the author made this word for the first time in dealing with the subject case) of snow-like fragrance by combining two words while Pacific Co., Ltd.'s mark, ICE SNOW, created a different concept 'BingSeol' (a coined Korean word; the author made this word for the first time in dealing with the subject case) of frozen snow. For this reason, the two marks are dissimilar in terms of appearance, pronunciation and concept."

After submitting the written brief, I focused on making this argument at the time of oral arguments before the Patent Court. I was very curious as to how the court would decide since I believed that my arguments were quite original and persuasive. Finally, a decision was issued in my client's favor. In adopting most of my arguments in its decision, the Patent Court stated:

"The subject registered trademark combines two words to produce a special concept of 'snow-like perfume or perfume made up of snow,' and thereby, has acquired a new distinctiveness. As such, we find that the subject registered trademark, when used on its designated goods, is deemed to possess the requisite special-purpose distinctiveness that functions to enable general consumers to indicate the source of the relevant goods. The subject registered trademark and the cited mark both are comprised of two English common words that can be understood by people with a junior high school level English. The word portions of both marks are not so intimately connected as to make it commercially unnatural to separate them. With this in mind, the words, PERFUME and SNOW, which comprise the subject registered trademark, and "SNOW" in the cited mark, are all functional indications that either lack distinctiveness or are substantially non-distinctive. Moreover, the word ICE contained in the cited mark likewise is perceived as "white as ice" or "pure" which constitute a functional indication directly indicating the characteristic (quality or efficacy) of its designated goods. When compared, both marks contain the word SNOW. However, because it constitutes a functional indication lacking distinctiveness, it cannot serve as the distinctive element."

"The similarity examination for the two marks cannot be achieved by separating them into its elements and comparing each element. Since separating the elements from each mark and determining the similarity of both marks is not appropriate in this case, we need to return to the basic test of comparing and determining similarity by reviewing the combined word marks in their entireties. When reviewing the subject registered mark and cited mark in their entireties and overall impressions, the appearance and pronunciation of both marks are dissimilar. Moreover, the subject registered mark represents a new concept of "snow perfume" or "snow fragrance," while the cited mark is perceived as a different new concept of "ice snow" or "frozen snow." For these reasons, the review of the two marks in their entireties show that they are dissimilar in terms of appearance, pronunciation and concept, and we do not find that general consumers will be confused or misled when used on identical or similar designated goods."

Just because the individual elements of a trademark lack distinctiveness, as was the case with my client's mark, the entire mark cannot be assumed to be non-distinctive. In this case, we prevailed on the argument that where the combination of two elements creates a new concept, the entire mark can have distinctiveness, and any determination of similarity between marks must also give consideration to the overall entirety of the marks.

"The client's mark, SNOW PERFUME, created a new concept of 'SeolHyang' "snow fragrance," while the other party's ICE SNOW created a new concept of 'BingSeol' "frozen snow."

Creating the original argument in this case and getting it acknowledged by the Patent Court is like sweet music to my ears.

2006 Huh (Dang) 5225

The Patent Court, 3rd Division Decision

Case No.: 2006 Huh 5225

Invalidation of Registration (Appellant) Plaintiff: Pacific Co., Ltd.

Plaintiff's Counsel: Patent Attorney Moon Soo Ha

Defendant: VOV Co., Ltd.

Defendant's Counsel: Patent Attorney Ho Hyun Nahm

Final Hearing: October 26, 2006

Date of Decision: November 23, 2006

ORDER

1. Plaintiff's claims shall be dismissed.
2. Costs of the action shall be borne by Plaintiff.

GIST OF CLAIM

The Original Decision as rendered by Korean Intellectual Property Tribunal on May 15, 2006 Case No. 2005 Dang 2560 shall be cancelled.

REASONS

1.   Details of the Original Decision which dismissed Plaintiff's request for invalidation of the subject registered trademark. [Evidence] Plaintiff's Evidence 1 and 2 with contents

A. Information on Defendant's subject registered trademark and cited mark

(1)   Defendant's subject registered trademark

(i)   Composition: SNOW PERFUME

(ii)   Reg. No.: 620752

(iii)   Filing Date/Registration Date: June 11, 2003/June 9, 2005

(iv)   Designated Goods: wood flavor, perfume, lavender products, shower cologne, eau du cologne (goods classification 3)

(2)   Cited mark

(i)   Composition: ICE SNOW

(ii)   Reg. No.: 512973

(iii)   Filing Date/Registration Date: August 21, 2000/February 20, 2002

(iv)   Designated Goods: lavender products, skin milk, cosmetic tissues, cosmetic soaps, shampoos, toothpastes, perfumes, lipsticks, eye shadows, manicures (goods classification 3)

B. Plaintiff's Action for Invalidation of Registration and Original Decision of Dismissal

(1)   Plaintiff filed an invalidation action against Defendant's subject registered trademark for the reason that Defendant's mark is identical or similar to the cited mark, which is Plaintiff's prior-registered trademark, and that both marks have identical or similar designated goods pursuant to Article 7(1)(7) of the Trademark Act.

(2)   On May 15, 2006, after reviewing Case No. 2005 Dang 2560, the Korean Intellectual Property Tribunal issued a decision dismissing Plaintiff's

claims after finding that two marks, when compared in their entireties, were not sufficiently similar to cause confusion or mislead consumers as to the source of the goods.

2. Plaintiff's Arguments for Cancellation of Original Decision and Related Issues

The main issue in this case lies in whether the subject registered mark falls within the scope of Article 6(1)(7) or Article 7(1)(7) of the Trademark Act. Plaintiff's gist of arguments on this point for cancellation of the Original Decision is as follows:

A. "PERFUME" portion of the subject registered mark is a generic term for perfumes and is not distinctive. When "SNOW" portion is used on designated goods, it lacks distinctiveness or is inadequately distinctive. Further, there are numerous registered marks that contain the term "SNOW," which renders this term inadequately distinctive. In this regard, the subject registered mark does not enable consumers to recognize whose goods it indicates in connection with a person's business and it also fails to indicate the source of the goods. For these reasons, the subject registration must be invalidated pursuant to Article 6(1)(7) of the Trademark Act.

B. Even if "SNOW" is considered to be distinctive, the subject registered mark and the cited mark are confusingly similar in that pronunciation and concept of both marks are identical when the SNOW portion of each mark is separated and compared. As such, the subject registered mark must be invalidated pursuant to Article 7(1)(7) of the Trademark Act.

3. Decision on Whether the Subject Registered Mark Falls Under the Scope of Article 6(1)(7) of the Trademark Act

A. Standards for determining distinctiveness under Article 6(1)(7) of the Trademark Act

The phrase "a mark which does not enable consumers to recognize whose goods it indicates in connection with a person's business other than those under sub-sections 1 through 6," as found in Article 6(1)(7) of the Trademark Act refers to a case where a mark that does not fall under the sub-sections 1 through 6 still may not be registered for lacking special distinctiveness to differentiate between one's mark and someone else's mark. As a result, whether a mark possesses special distinctiveness is determined based on whether a general consumer can recognize the source of a product in relation to the mark itself (Korean Supreme Court, June 23, 2005, Decision No. 2004 Hu 2871).

B. Whether the subject registered mark has distinctiveness

The subject registered mark is a word mark that combines English words "SNOW" and "PERFUME." The PERFUME portion lacks distinctiveness when used on its designated goods as it is a generic term for products or is merely a functional indication. Moreover, the dictionary meaning of SNOW is "snow, pure white," so when it is used on its designated goods "perfume, lavender types", general consumers would perceive it as "as white as snow," "clean, pure," which renders it a functional indication that directly describes the characteristic (quality or effect) of the designated goods. Not only that, there are numerous prior-registered marks that contain the term "SNOW" (Defendant's exhibits 4-1 through 4-20), and as a result, any distinctiveness in the word SNOW is negligible.

However, the subject registered mark combines two words to create a new and special concept of "SeolHyang" "snow perfume" or "snow fragrance" which together possess distinctiveness.

For these reasons, we find that the subject registered mark, when used on its designated goods, enables a general consumer to indicate the source of such goods, and as such, that it possesses the requisite special distinctiveness as a trademark.

4.　Decision on Whether the Subject Registered Mark Falls Under the Scope of Article 7(1)(7) of the Trademark Act

A. Principle of reviewing a mark in its entirety

Trademarks are used to distinguish between one's products and others so as to prevent misunderstanding or confusion as to the source of the goods. It functions generally with the entirety of the mark working as a single unit. As such, the fundamental principle in the determination as to the similarity of two marks is that the analysis must be based on the entireties of two marks in terms of their respective appearance, pronunciation and concept.

When conducting an analysis of the marks in their entireties, if a particular element in a mark is found to attract the attention of the consumers and if the distinctiveness of the mark is only recognized because of that particular element, a determination of similarity can be made by separating out the central distinctive element and analyzing the functional nature of the mark in comparing the two marks in parallel with the analysis of the marks in their entireties. But it should be noted that such analysis of the element may only be used as a way to arrive at an appropriate analysis of the marks in their entireties (Korean Supreme Court, May 24, 1994, Decision No. 94 Hu 265).

B. Whether the Subject Registered Mark and the Cited Mark are Similar

(1) Comparing appearance

The subject registered mark is comprised of two English words, "SNOW" and "PERFUME," while the cited mark likewise comprises two English words, "Ice" and "Snow." Comparing two marks in their entireties, their appearance is dissimilar.

(2) Comparing pronunciation and concept

The subject registered mark and the cited mark are comprised of two commonly used English words which are understood with a junior high school level education. The word portions of both marks are not so intimately connected as to make it commercially unnatural to separate them. With this in mind, the words, PERFUME and SNOW, which comprise the subject registered trademark, and "Snow" in the cited mark, are all functional indications that either lack distinctiveness or are substantially non-distinctive. Moreover, the word "Ice" contained in the cited mark likewise is perceived as "white as ice" or "pure" which constitute a functional indication directly indicating the characteristic (quality or efficacy) of its designated goods.

When compared, both marks contain the word SNOW. However, because it constitutes a functional indication lacking distinctiveness, it cannot serve as the distinctive element. Accordingly, it is inappropriate to determine the similarity of the two marks by separating them into their particular elements and analyzing them.

(3) Determination of similarity based on analysis of the marks' entireties

Since it is inappropriate to determine the similarity of the two marks by separating them into their particular elements and analyzing them, we need to return to the fundamental approach of analyzing and determining similarity based on the combined word marks in their entireties.

In comparing the totality and entirety of the subject registered mark and the cited mark, their respective appearance and pronunciation are dissimilar. Moreover, the subject registered mark represents a new concept of "SeolHyang" "snow perfume" or "snow fragrance," while the cited mark is perceived as a different new concept of "BingSeol" "ice snow" or "frozen snow."

For these reasons, the review of the two marks in their entireties shows that they are dissimilar in terms of appearance, pronunciation and concept, and we do not find that general consumers will be confused or misled when used on identical or similar designated goods.

5. Conclusion

Based on the above, the subject registered mark does not fall under either Article 6(1)(7) or Article 7(1)(7), and the Original Decision which rendered this finding is correct. Having found that Plaintiff's claim for reversal of the Original Decision are without proper basis, this court hereby decides as stated in the Order.

Presiding Judge Yong Ho Moon
Judge Young Chul Suh
Judge Tae Shik Yoon

THE GUARDIAN ANGEL FOR THE BRITISH ROYAL CHIEF DESIGNER'S TRADEMARK

-Dispute involving Sir Hardy Amies' brand -

For 107 years, "Austin Reed" has been a famous U.K. brand which long enjoyed a loyal following of enthusiasts who praise and love brand's highest quality products and who love its high-class sense of style.

Its products exemplify a serene and flowing sense of tradition with the highest quality materials and inimitable and unique attention to detail. By combining a modern feel to a comfortable but individualistic design, the brand continues to capture the imagination of its customers worldwide.

Austin Reed began exporting its products throughout the world since 1929 and currently operates about 45 shops and 30 distribution centers in the U.K. With licensing partnerships throughout the world, including Korea, U.S., Japan, Singapore, Russia and Indonesia, Austin Reed products are currently available in over 1,000 shops.

Sir Hardy Amies was the chief fashion designer for Queen Elizabeth of the British royal family. He established his own company, Hardy Amies Ltd., to pursue his own brand business and began to conduct business throughout the world. With his worldwide popularity, he enjoyed a successful licensing business after registering his trademarks on all fashion-related items, including apparel from which he was earning substantial royalties.

As opposed to having his products directly manufactured and sold in Korea, his company engaged in providing product manufacturing guidelines on the designs and product materials pursuant to a license agreement. Korean companies manufactured and sold Hardy Amies'products in accordance with such guidelines and paid royalties as consideration. Along the way, the trademark licensees for Korea changed a few times. This would happen when the contract was up for renewal or when the contract was terminated due to the breach by a licensee.

It goes without saying that acquiring trademark registration and maintaining its validity are critical to a licensing business. But how could this happen? There was a challenge to cancel the trademark registration for Hardy Amies trademark! A close friend of mine who was a U.K. patent attorney working at a major U.K. intellectual property law firm sought my advice.

A former licensee whose contract had been terminated due to their breach was found to have continued to produce and sell products bearing Hardy Amies trademark. When Hardy Amies Ltd. filed a trademark infringement lawsuit against the former licensee, they in turn filed a trademark cancellation action.

The basis for their cancellation action was that Hardy Amies trademark was not used in Korea for three years. To my surprise, they had lost in the first instance before the Korean Intellectual Property Tribunal, and the case was now before the Patent Court. What's worse, when I reviewed the case, it looked like they would lose again.

If their trademark registration were to be cancelled, not only would they not be entitled to prevent the former Korean licensee from infringing the mark, they would not be able to assert any trademark rights over any company or individual who uses the Hardy Amies trademark. Inevitably, the Hardy Amies' licensing business in Korea would simply evaporate. The client then asked,

"How could we have lost in the non-use cancellation action and now be on the verge of losing in the Patent Court when we actively used the registered trademark in Korea?"

Even though the client in fact used their trademark in Korea actively through their local licensee, they had not registered their licensee with the Patent Office, as required by the Trademark Act in effect at the time. It is true that a non-use cancellation action can be successfully defended because use of a mark by an unregistered licensee is recognized as a proper use of the trademark.

However, the problem was in the fact that the Trademark Act also provided at the time a provision that subjected a registered trademark to cancellation if the owner of the registered trademark allowed a third party to use the registered trademark for more than 6 months without registering the license. It would appear that the cancellation based on non-use can be avoided if evidence of trademark use by the unregistered licensee is presented. But this would ultimately lead to the loss of trademark registration because submitting evidence of trademark use by the unregistered licensee is tantamount to admission of trademark use by an unregistered licensee.

Out of urgency, the legal counsel representing the company had already submitted evidence of trademark use by an unregistered licensee as he determined that it was more important to prevail on the pending cancellation action for now. Not submitting anything would have automatically led to cancellation for non-use. It was at this juncture that my U.K. patent attorney friend sought my advice. He wanted to see if there was any way to salvage the trademark registration.

"What possibly can I do under these circumstances?"

With that thought in mind, I started searching for a solution. I concluded that there was a solution. I had found a way to maintain the registration without relying on the local licensee's use.

Under the Trademark Act, use of trademark in advertising is also recognized as trademark use. Previously, I had worked on a non-use cancellation action with a colleague attorney when representing Guess, Inc., a world famous fashion company. That was indeed a case in which we successfully argued before the Supreme Court that advertisements for the trademark featured in foreign publications were proper evidence of use in Korea if such publications were distributed in Korea. I presented my opinion with confidence.

"There certainly is a way to keep the registration. Look for foreign fashion publications that contained advertisements featuring Hardy Amies brand. If we can show that any of those publications were actually and legitimately distributed in Korea, we should be able to defend against the non-use cancellation action without relying on the licensee's evidence of use."

The client was overjoyed with my opinion.

"That is wonderful news. There must be something. We'll find it and send it right away."

This case, which had been represented by a different law firm, was promptly transferred to our office. About a week passed. An extremely disappointing message was faxed in.

"We looked everywhere, but couldn't find it."

Nonetheless, I was pretty certain that a brand such as Hardy Amies would have had its advertisements featured in international fashion magazines. I instructed all my staff members to comb through all the major bookstores as well as used bookstores. This wasn't even something the client requested. The telephone rang, and I was met with the scream of an out of breath voice of our trademark manager.

"We found it! We found Hardy Amies advertisement featured in a Japanese fashion magazine called 'The Great Illustrated Guide to Men's First Class Luxury Goods'."

We achieved this result by maintaining a sliver of hope and diligently searching from bookstore to bookstore while facing a desperate situation and a certain defeat. Even the client itself could not do anything to help. Our staff members were elated.

It goes without saying that the clients were even more excited upon receiving our report that we found the use evidence.

We filed our arguments based on this use evidence and appropriately applying the prior cases. We also submitted the prior Supreme Court case on the non-use cancellation action involving Guess, Inc.'s trademark which ruled that advertisements carrying the subject mark featured in a foreign publication is sufficient use evidence if the publication is distributed in Korea.

An issue still remained. It was in the form of the prior counsel's written brief in which he argued that the trademark was used based on the submitted trademark use evidence by an unregistered licensee.

Fortunately, a hearing had not taken place since the submission of the previously-submitted brief, which meant that we could withdraw it along with the attached evidence. With this in place, as expected, the Patent Court reversed the Original Decision by declaring that the foreign publication we found containing Hardy Amies advertisement constituted proper evidence of trademark use. The other party then filed an appeal to the Supreme Court, but that effort was futile.

This was the moment where we successfully overcame the desperate situation of almost losing the trademark registration for Hardy Amies and its entire Korean business. I hope the readers can also imagine the great sense of satisfaction that I had in communicating this wonderful news to the client.

The client as well as the U.K. patent attorney who entrusted this case to me both sent their roaring celebratory messages. In the process of creatively using an advertisement featured in a foreign publication as evidence of use and undertaking a sweeping search of bookstores, even though the client had not even asked for it, this experience again reminded me how much difference one can make by giving your best effort and believing in the slightest of possibilities. I will forever keep the memory of this case close to my heart.

Korean Supreme Court Decision, Division 1
Case No: 98 Hu 1907 Cancellation of registration (Supreme Court)
Plaintiff, Respondent: Hardy Amies Ltd.
Plaintiff's Counsel: Sukho Seo, Esq., Ho Hyun Nahm, Patent Attorney
Defendant, Appellant: Lee ____
Defendant's Counsel: Sejin Law Office, PC.
Defendant's Counsel: Byungryul Lee, Donghak Lee, Hongki Min, Songho Park
Original Decision: Patent Court, September 4, 1998, Decision 98 Huh 867

ORDER

The appeal to the Supreme Court is dismissed. Costs of the appeal shall be borne by the defendant.

REASONS

The Original Decision found that Daedongbangjik Co., Ltd, a Japanese importer, had published an advertisement featuring the products bearing the subject registered mark in the 1993, 1994 and 1995 editions of "The Great Illustrated Guide to Men's First Class Luxury Goods", as published by Kangchulsa Co., Ltd. and that said publication had been imported and sold by a local bookstore around the time of their publication. It then held that this is deemed as advertising or otherwise publication of the subject registered mark in Korea, which constitutes use of trademark required under Article 2(1)(6) of the old Trademark Act (prior to amendment of Law 5355 enacted on August 22, 1997), and thus, the subject registered mark does not fall under the scope of Article 73(1)(3) of the same Act which defines a cause for cancellation of a registered mark. In our review, we find that the Original Decision is correct and that it does not violate any rule of evidence, lack adequate review or misunderstand the applicable law. For this reason, all of the reasons for appeal are denied. We hereby dismiss the appeal, and assess the costs of this action in accordance with the Order.

March 23, 1999

Presiding Justice: Chief Justice Sung Taik Shin

Justice: Joon Suh Park

Justice: Im Soo Lee

Coordinating Justice: Sung Suh

HYUNDAI MOTOR COMPANY PREVAILS OVER THE LOTUS GROUP OF U.K.

-LOTS vs. LOTUS-

As counsel for Hyundai Motor Company, I had filed a trademark application for registration for LOTS for use on cars. The application passed examination without complication, and registration was issued when no opposition was filed against it during the opposition period. One day, however, Group Lotus PLC, a U.K. car company, filed an invalidation action against Hyundai Motor's LOTS trademark registration.

"It is similar to Lotus PLC's prior-registered mark, LOTUS, in connection with cars. The registration must be invalidated since it shouldn't have been issued a registration in the first place."

At first glance, Lotus's argument appeared to have a point. The only difference between the two marks was the presence of U, as such, there was similarity in appearance. In terms of pronunciation, which examination is generally given more weight in determining similarity of marks, Hyundai Motor's registered mark LOTS and Lotus'prior-registered mark LOTUS sound sufficiently similar to cause confusion among consumers. Those arguments were plausible.

But I approached it methodically. Despite their argument, the presence of the English alphabet U in the cited mark should support the argument that they are dissimilar in terms of appearance. The problem was in pronunciation. Lotus had submitted a Korean classical literature that showed that Hyundai Motor's registered mark, LOTS, was pronounced "loh-teuh-seuh".

Nonetheless, I had a different opinion.

"That word may have been pronounced that way a long time ago. However, in today's world where average educational level is higher than junior high, the average consumer today is someone who has more than a junior high education. LOTS is an English word that serves as a plural form of the word LOT, which has the meaning of a name of bird, share, and a unit. As a noun, it is used to indicate many things and variety, and as an adverb, very and many. It is pronounced either "lahts" or "lohts." Accordingly, it cannot be similar to LOTUS, whose pronunciation is "lo-tus" and is without any specific. The subject registered mark cannot be invalidated as it was validly registered notwithstanding Lotus' LOTUS mark already having been registered."

I made my arguments in this regard. I also gave an example.

"How ridiculous would it sound if the plural form of the word CAT were pronounced as "ka-teuh-seuh"? How many people would pronounce the phrase "a lots of" as "a-loh-teuh-seuh-oh-beuh"?"

In so doing, I submitted the 1986 version of "Public Notification on the Standards of Foreign Language Markings" which indicates the pronunciation of "ts" as "cheu". Litigation is a battle of evidence. This argument was accepted in its entirety by the Korean Intellectual Property Tribunal, and we were able to successfully defend the invalidation action.

The other side immediately filed an appeal to the Patent Court seeking to cancel the Original Decision. To my surprise, the Patent Court decided in favor of Lotus.

"As a colloquial term, LOTS is a word that is used with another English word in the form of "lots of +", and as such, it is presented in capital letters in countries like Korea whose native language is not English. When used by itself, we cannot conclusively conclude that LOTS will always be perceived in its true meaning and be pronounced in its English phonetics. We need to consider the fact that LOT is described as "loh-teu" in Korea and that good portion of our consumers or dealers are not very familiar with English phonetics, and as such, it would not be unusual to simply add the sound "s" to "loh-teu" in pronouncing "LOTS."

The Patent Court had reversed the Korean Intellectual Property Tribunal's Original Decision, which was in our favor, based on its reasoning that when the subject registered mark is pronounced as "loh-teu-seu", it is identical or similar in pronunciation with the prior-registered mark "loh-tus" or "loh-toos." I could not accept such finding by the Patent Court, so I filed an appeal to the Supreme Court.

"The evidence presented in the Original Decision is insufficient to acknowledge that LOTS would be generally pronounced by consumers and dealers in our country as "loh-teu-seu." On the contrary, according to Foreign Language Markings in the Ministry of Education's Public Notification No. 85-11 (January 7, 1986), [ts] before a consonant or a final consonant is to be described as "cheu", and for these reasons, it is more likely that most of the consumers or dealers in Korea will pronounce LOTS as "lahts" or "lohts." When the subject registered mark is pronounced as "lahts" or "lohts", both marks are significantly dissimilar in pronunciation, and as such, they cannot be considered similar in their entireties. We find that the Original Decision, which decided to the contrary, has failed to properly review the issue of how general consumers and dealers would pronounce the subject registered mark and this failure has affected the outcome of the decision. The appellant's arguments in this regard have merit."

The Supreme Court so declared, and then reversed and remanded the Patent Court's decision.

There's almost no perfect principle or standard in this world. Almost everything always changes. For this reason, we must always adapt to the changes in the environment. Likewise, the standards for determining similarity must also adapt to the changing consumers. The true value and significance of this Supreme Court case was it acknowledged my argument that the English proficiency level for average Korean consumers have progressed.

Korean Supreme Court, September 30, 2005, Decision 2004 Hu 2628
[Invalidation of Registration (Appeal to Supreme Court)] [unpublished]

[Decided Issue]

(1) Standards for determining similarity of word marks

(2) A case that ruled that registered mark LOTS and prior cited mark LOTUS were not considered to be similar due to distinctive difference in pronunciation

[Cited Statute]

(1) Trademark Act, Article 7(1)(7)

(2) Trademark Act, Article 7(1)(7)

[Cited Case]

(1) Korean Supreme Court, February 25, 2000, Decision 97 Hu 3050 (Gong 200 Sang, 848) Korean Supreme Court, October 10, 2003, Decision 2003 Hu 816

[Full Text]

[Plaintiff, Respondent] Group Lotus PLC (Counsel, Young Dong Mok, Patent Attorney and 2 others)

[Defendant, Appellant] Hyundai Motor Company (Counsel, Ho Hyun Nahm, Patent Attorney)

[Original Decision] Patent Court, July 30, 2004, Decision 2003 Huh 7411

[Order]

Original Decision is reversed, and this case is remanded to the Patent Court.

[Reasons]

1. Gist of the Original Decision

According to the Reasons for the Original Decision, it compared "LOTS", the subject registered mark in this case (trademark registration no. 541541), with its prior-registered mark, "LOTUS" ("cited mark"); both marks are slightly dissimilar based on the presence or non-presence of the letter "U", but otherwise have similar appearance given the identical four letters placed in the same order; the subject registered mark, has a letter S added to its singular form LOT, which has the meaning of a name of bird, share, fate, a unit, location and group; as a noun, it is used to indicate "many things" and "variety", and as an adverb, "very and many;" if the subject registered mark were perceived in its dictionary meaning of "many things" and "variety," then it could be said that it is pronounced as "lahts" or "lohts"; however, LOTS is a colloquial term where it is used with another English word in the form of "lots of + a noun", and as such, it is presented in capital letters in countries like Korea whose native language is not English; when used by itself, it cannot be conclusively concluded that LOTS will always be perceived in its true meaning and be pronounced in English phonetics; given that LOT is described as "loh-teu" in Korea and that good portion of our consumers or dealers are not very familiar with English phonetics, and as such, it would not be unusual to simply add the sound "s" to "loh-teu" in pronouncing LOTS; if the subject registered mark is pronounced as "loh-teu-seu", then its pronunciation is identical with or similar to the cited mark; in terms of concept, it would be difficult to conclude that general consumers would be able to distinguish the subject registered mark "LOTS" from the prior registered cited mark "LOTUS" based on the general level of English proficiency in Korea, which means that both marks are not comparable in terms of concept; and for these reasons, the Original Decision held that the subject registered mark and the cited mark are considered to be similar marks in their entireties.

2. The Court's Decision

We, however, find the decision of the Original Decision to be unacceptable.

A. In determining similarity of the trademarks, a decision must be made on the basis of whether they can mislead or confuse the consumers of the trademarks by conducting an analysis of the marks in their entireties and how the marks are recalled. They cannot be considered similar if the marks in their entireties can clearly avoid misleading or confusion as to the source among the public even if any one of appearance, pronunciation or concept is deemed similar. Similarly, the marks must be deemed similar if there is sufficient similarity in pronunciation or concept that would likely mislead or confuse consumers as to the source of goods even if there are dissimilar elements between the two. Given the wide distribution of today's media and advertising modes, where telephones and other voice-dependent channels are frequently utilized, the most important element in determining similarity of word marks would be the element of pronunciation (refer to Korean Supreme Court, February 25, 2000, Decision 97 Hu 3050).

B. Based on the above principle and record, the subject registered trademark and cited mark have similarity in terms of appearance. However, the evidence presented in the Original Decision is insufficient to acknowledge that "LOTS" would be generally pronounced by consumers and dealers in our country as "loh-teu-seu." On the contrary, according to Foreign Language Markings in the Ministry of Education's Public Notification No. 85-11 (January 7, 1986), [ts] before a consonant or a final consonant is to be described as "cheu", and for these reasons, there is more probability that most of the consumers or dealers in Korea will pronounce "LOTS" as "lahts" or "lohts." When the subject registered mark is pronounced as "lahts" or "lohts", both marks are significantly dissimilar in pronunciation, and as such, both marks cannot be considered similar in their entireties. We find that the Original Decision, which decided to the contrary, has failed to properly review the issue of how general consumers and dealers would pronounce the subject registered mark and this failure has affected the outcome of the decision. The appellant's arguments in this regard have merit.

3. Therefore, we reverse the Original Decision and remand this case back to the Patent Court for review and decision. We unanimously decide as provided in the Order.

Chief Justice Yong Dam Kim (Presiding Justice)

Ji Dahm Yoo, Ki Won Bae (Coordinating Justices)

Kang Kook Lee

(Source: Korean Supreme Court, September 30, 2005, Decision 2004 Hu 2628 [Invalidation of Registration (Appeal to Supreme Court)] General Legal Information Gazette

ELEGANCE IS REBORN AS A VALUED TRADEMARK

Established in 1930, the fashion company Elegance GmbH began exporting apparel to France, Austria, Swiss and other European countries in the 1960s. They opened their own brand stores in Japan in 1970, Taiwan in 1980 and Hong Kong in 1985.

In Korea, they opened their imported luxury good shop in 1980 under the name, "Elegance Boutique," featuring their own manufactured goods. By 1995, they had eight shops including Seoul, Pusan and Kwangju where they sold goods designed and manufactured by Elegance.

Starting many decades ago, Elegance regularly published fashion magazines known as "Elegance Boutique" and "Elegance Paris" and has sold them in Korea and throughout the world through a number of outlets. In those magazines, they used their cited mark by itself, or in combination with other indications, such as Elegance PARIS, Elégance or PARIS æ. Elegance's "Elegance" magazine was first brought into Korea in December 1968, and they were imported on a regular basis from 1973 to December 1992 and distributed in Korea and enjoyed by a number of fashion dealers and consumers in Korea.

Like Hardy Amies, Ltd., Elegance was engaged in an active licensing business in Korea. But, their former licensee who had been terminated for breach of the license agreement was again causing the trouble. They were using a mark, "Hanyoung Elegance," which combined their company name, Hanyoung" with "Elegance" by manufacturing and selling goods bearing that mark.

Their conduct was sufficient to mislead consumers into thinking that these were products manufactured by a joint venture between Elegance and Hanyoung Industries Co., Ltd. The owners of the registered mark, Elegance, would not stand for it. They issued a cease and desist letter to Hangyoung Co., Ltd., their former licensee, to immediately cease and desist from infringing the trademark rights of Elegance. Hanyoung Industries Co., Ltd. simply ignored it as if nothing happened and continued to use the mark. Having no choice, Elegance filed a lawsuit against them.

Much to our surprise, Hanyoung Industries Co., Ltd. showed that they owned the trademark registration to the mark "Hanyoungelegance and Hanyoung Elegance in Korean." They argued that this is simply a proper use of their own registered trademark and they are not engaged in infringing Elegance's trademark rights.

Unless we invalidated their registered mark, it appeared that we could not prevail in the infringement action. However, invalidating their registered mark appeared to be an insurmountable task. Since "Elegance" meant grace and classy, it was a mark that lacked distinctiveness in relation to fashion products, and this meant that it could be used by anyone. The Supreme Court had already held, in two different cases, that this word could not be registered as a trademark for this very reason.

In other words, the word "Elegance" lacks distinctiveness, and as such, determination of similarity between this mark and another mark must take place without considering that non-distinctive portion. This is because no one should be able to exercise exclusive trademark rights over that non-distinctive portion, regardless of who holds the registration itself. It was definitely not an easy fight.

At first, there seemed no way out. But to the client, this was a desperate situation. If we didn't prevail on the invalidation action, Elegance becomes a mark that anyone can use, which meant that their Korean licensing business would collapse.

Most general consumers in Korea simply assume that Elegance is a well-known foreign fashion company, which indicated to me that the name certainly serves to function as a trademark. I asked myself, why is that? I concluded that the answer was because the mark possesses distinctiveness through use. In other words, it lacked distinctiveness because it initially was defined only by its meaning of "grace and classy." However, when Elegance was exclusively used for a long time, it acquired a new significance as a trademark of a specific company.

I reviewed the two prior Korean Supreme Court cases, and I found that the counsel representing Elegance in those cases never argued the point of acquiring distinctiveness through use. I was relieved.

"It doesn't matter that the Supreme Court decided, in two separate cases, that Elegance lacks distinctiveness as a trademark. Our chances of success are good if we argue distinctiveness based on use as a new factual position."

I sent this comment to the client, and the client proceeded accordingly. Of course, we still needed to prove the fact that Korean consumers perceive Elegance as a trademark of a specific company through continuous and exclusive use in Korea in order to prevail on the "distinctiveness based on use" ('secondary meaning' or 'acquired distinctiveness') argument.

However, upon receiving and analyzing the materials that client sent for use as evidence of notoriety of the mark in Korea, we found them to be grossly deficient. After much pondering, our staff once again were dispatched to used bookstores and foreign bookstores as well as importers.

We found that the fashion magazine "Elegance" had been imported and sold in Korea for over 30 years and that almost all of the fashion designers were subscribers to this magazine. We were able to collect lots of materials for use as evidence showing not only that luxury goods bearing the Elegance trademark were imported and sold, but that the mark was actively used by a number of licensees. This time again, the client had not requested that we conduct a search of local bookstores and foreign publication importers.

We filed an invalidation action against the trademark registration of Hanyoung Industries Co., Ltd.'s "Hanyoungelegance + Hanyoung Elegance in Korean." As evidence of distinctiveness based on use, we submitted the materials collected from our search of used bookstores and book importers.

"The word, Elegance, possesses distinctiveness, and the subject registered mark which contains the word Elegance is similar to the famous trademark owned by Elegance company and the prior-registered cited mark because they cause confusion as to the source and quality of the goods. As such, it must be invalidated."

I argued forcefully. However, the Korean Intellectual Property Tribunal did not agree with me. The trial examiner must have been weary of the fact that there have already been two Supreme Court cases which ruled that Elegance is non-distinctive and that there had been practically no case acknowledging distinctiveness based on use even though the law contained a specific provision for such situation.

We filed an appeal to the Patent Court, seeking cancellation of the Original Decision. The Patent Court was different. They ruled in my favor. They had acknowledged that the word Elegance had distinctiveness as a trademark. Not only were we able to successfully invalidate someone else's trademark registration that contained the word "Elegance," we also made it impossible for anyone to use the word Elegance as a mark without distinctiveness.

Actually, too many attorneys and patent attorneys feel constrained by Supreme Court decisions. Often, they say that it is too difficult or nearly impossible to win because of the Supreme Court decisions. For certain factual situations, that is of course true. Justice by its nature, however, is not something that can be uniformly or universally defined that easily. Each case can have some different factual relationship that can be distinguished from prior cases.

No matter how well-established, even a Supreme Court precedent can be overcome by identifying a different element and applying it to the unique facts and circumstances of the case at hand - and then you can say "justice!" A Supreme Court decision should not always be looked at as the standard bearer of the best available justice. The ultimate goal should be the pursuit of justice that applies to each case.

Patent Court, Division 2 Decision

2002 Huh 888 Invalidation of Registration (Sang)

Plaintiff: Elegance Rolf Offergelt GmbH

Plaintiff's Counsel: Ho Hyun Nahm, Patent Attorney

Defendant: Hanyoung Industries Co., Ltd.

Defendant's Counsel: Changjo Law Firm Jung Hwan Moon, Esq.

Final Hearing: June 21, 2002

ORDER

1. Korean Intellectual Property Tribunal's Decision dated December 28, 2001 (2001 Dang 1264) is hereby cancelled.

2. Costs of litigation shall be borne by the Defendant.

GIST OF CLAIM

As decided in the Order.

REASONS

1. Background Information

[Recognized basis: Full gist of arguments and contents of Plaintiff's Ex. 1, 2]

A. Information on the subject registered mark

(1) Registration Number: 343058

(2) Registrant: Defendant

(3) Filing date/Date on which Registration was Decided/Registration Date: March 24, 1993/ June 29, 1996/ July 16, 1996

(4) Mark: 한영엘레강스
Hanyungelegance

(5) Designated Goods: Umbrella, paper umbrella, parasol, beach parasol, umbrella cover, umbrella shaft [old Trademark Act, Enforcement Regulations (prior to Ministry of Commerce and Industry Regulations No. 83, February 23, 1998, Attachment 1 to Article 6(1) Class 27)

B. Original Decision

(1) Plaintiff argues that the subject registered mark and its major portion is similar to "Elegance" ("cited mark"), which is an abbreviated name for Plaintiff company and also a well-known mark; that use of the subject registered mark will fall under Articles 7(1)(6) and 7(1)(9) and 7(1)(10) of the Trademark Act by misleading Korean consumers into thinking that it is related to Plaintiff's mark that is well-known in Korea and internationally; that the use of the subject registered mark in connection with Plaintiff's line of business or designated goods such as "umbrellas" will fall under Article 7(1)(11) of the Trademark Act in that it would cause confusion among and mislead consumers; and for these reasons, that the subject registered mark must be invalidated.

(2) The Korean Intellectual Property Tribunal reviewed this case no. 2001 Dang 1264 and issued a decision dismissing the Plaintiff's claims on December 28, 2001.

C. Gist of the Original Decision's Reasons

(1) Whether the Cited Mark is Well-Known and Element of Distinctiveness

While it is true that the cited mark is registered for magazines in about 10 countries, there are no materials to help determine how, for how long and under what method, it was used in Korea. As such, it cannot be said objectively that the cited mark is famous and well-known among general consumers and dealers.

Moreover, the cited mark has the meaning of "elegance, class, intelligence, style" according to the French dictionary, and unless it is combined with another element that is distinctive or has acquired distinctiveness through use, it does not have distinctiveness as a trademark.

(2) Whether the subject registered mark falls under Articles 7(1)(6) and 7(1)(9) and 7(1)(10) of the Trademark Act

Whether a mark falls under the above-cited provision is determined by the fact that the mark is deemed a famous mark, that it is well-known to consumers or that consumers and dealers readily perceive the mark or goods bearing the mark to be the mark or goods bearing the mark of a specific person or company. The cited mark does not fall under any of these situations, and as such, the subject registered mark clearly does not fall under the above provision without the need to examine the similarity of the marks.

2.   Arguments of the Parties

A. Plaintiff's Reasons to Cancel the Original Decision

(1) The subject registered mark contains "Elegance" which is an abbreviated name for Plaintiff company's famous company. Because Defendant filed for and registered this mark without Plaintiff's consent, Article 7(1)(6) of the Trademark Act applies.

(2) The subject registered mark is similar to the cited mark, which was already well-known to consumers as indicating Plaintiff's products prior to the filing of the application for registration of the subject registered mark. Thus, the subject registered mark falls under Article 7(1)(9) of the Trademark as a mark designated goods which are identical or similar to those of the cited mark.

(3) The subject registered mark is likely to cause confusion or be perceived as being in a joint venture relationship, license relationship or other special relationship with Plaintiff, and as such, it is likely to confuse or mislead consumers as to the quality of the goods pursuant to Articles 7(1)(10) and 7(1)(11).

B. Defendant's Arguments

(1) Cited mark has not been registered in Korea, and it is an unregistrable mark by itself.

(2) When considering the use of the cited mark in Korea, distribution of its products, and the time, method, and form of its business activities, the cited mark does not constitute a well-known mark in Korea.

3. Decision

A. The Extent to Which the Cited Mark is Known in the Relevant Industry

[Basis of Proof: Plaintiff's Ex. 3, 4-1 thru 4-3, 5, 6, 20, 29, 32-1 thru 32-30, 33-1 thru 33-6, 38-1 thru 38-3, and its contents and related arguments]

(1) Established in 1930, Plaintiff began exporting to France, Austria, Switzerland and other European countries in the 1960s and opened their own brand stores in Japan in 1970, Taiwan in 1980 and Hong Kong in 1985. In Korea, they opened their imported luxury good shop in 1980 under the name, "Elegance Boutique" featuring Plaintiff's own manufactured goods, and by 1995, they had eight shops including Seoul, Pusan and Kwangju where they sold goods designed and manufactured by Plaintiff.

(2) Many decades before the trademark application for the subject registered mark was filed on March 24, 1993, Plaintiff had been publishing fashion magazines known as "Elegance Boutique," and "Elegance Paris" on a regular basis and have been selling them in Korea and throughout the world through a number of outlets [Elegance Boutique published its celebratory 25th Anniversary 148th Edition version in 1995 (Plaintiff's Ex. 5)]. These magazines featured the cited mark itself or in combination with Elegance PARIS, Elégance or PARIS æ which were used on apparel, shoes, bags and accessories which were designed and manufactured by Plaintiff. Plaintiff's "Elegance" magazine was first brought into Korea in December 1968, and they were imported two to four times a year with each order numbering 500 to 2,000 magazines from 1973 to December 1992 and distributed in Korea and enjoyed by a number of fashion dealers and consumers in Korea. During this period, the total value of the imported publications amounted to almost $180,000. On Page 115 of the 1993 139th Edition of Elegance PARIS, we note especially that a full-page advertisement in Korean was featured.

(3) Prior to the filing of the application for the subject registered mark, Plaintiff had already registered about 20 marks identical to the cited mark or marks that contained the cited mark in many countries around the world, designating "umbrella, parasol, apparel, shoes, textile, accessories, glasses, jewelry, bag, leather goods, cosmetics and magazines." In Korea, Plaintiff filed for and registered the mark "Elegance HOMME" on apparel, gloves, accessories as designated goods. (Filed on November 27, 1987, Registered on July 6, 1989).

(4) The mark "𝕏ELEGANCE" was already included in the "Collection of Registered Foreign Well-Known Marks" for apparel and bags as published by the Korean Intellectual Property Office (KIPO) in 1986. Based on its own market research, KIPO also published "Collection of Foreign Trademarks" which also featured "Elegance HOMME" for apparel.

B. Acquisition of Distinctiveness by the Cited Mark

In the French-Korean dictionary (Samhwa Publications, April 30, 1994), the cited mark is defined as "elegance, style." Similarly, "elegance", which is similar to the cited mark, is defined as "elegant, graceful diction", and as such, it does have the characteristic of a descriptive indication. However, at the very least, as the acknowledged facts indicate, by the date of June 29, 1996 when the decision to grant registration to the subject registered mark was made, it is appropriate to conclude that the cited mark had already acquired distinctiveness.

C. Whether the Subject Registered Mark and Cited Mark are Similar

The subject registered mark is a mark that combines the Korean words "Hanyoungelegance" situated on top of the Roman letters "Hanyoungelegance." Since the elements of the subject registered mark are not so intimately connected as to make it unnatural to divide it into its elements, this mark can be divided into its two elements, "Hanyoung" or "Elegance," for the purpose of comparing its pronunciation and concept.

In this regard, if the subject registered mark is perceived as "elegance" in Korea or "elegance" in English, it is identical or similar to the cited mark in terms of pronunciation and concept, and as such, two marks are similar in their entireties.

D. Whether the Subject Registered Mark Falls under Article 7(1)(6) of the Trademark Act

Although the "elegance" portion of the subject registered mark can be said to constitute the same abbreviated term for Plaintiff's company name, it cannot be said that "elegance," as the abbreviated term for Plaintiff's company name, had attained the level of well-known mark in Korea by the time the application for the subject registered mark was filed in view of the acknowledged facts regarding the period of use, method, form and scope of activities of the same company name. For this reason, the subject registered mark does not fall under Article 7(1)(6) of the Trademark Act.

E. Whether the Subject Registered Mark Falls under Articles 7(1)(9) and 7(1)(10) of the Trademark Act

If the cited mark is to invalidate the registration of the subject registered mark on the basis of its status as a well-known and famous mark under Articles 7(1)(9) and 7(1)(10) of the Trademark Act, it is necessary to show that the cited mark was readily perceived by the consumers or dealers as a mark used by a specific source at the time the application for the subject registered mark was filed. Based on the acknowledged facts that deal with use of the cited mark until the date of such application, March 24, 1993, we cannot find that the cited mark was a well-known or famous mark by that time. As such, the subject registered mark does not fall under either article referenced above.

F. Whether the Subject Registered Mark Falls under Article 7(1)(11)of the Trademark Act

(1) We now review whether the cited mark is so well-known among the general consumers and dealers in Korea that they would perceive such mark or

goods bearing that mark to be those of a specific source. Based on the above acknowledged facts, including the extent to which the products bearing the cited mark were advertised, the history of the business activities and scope of use of the cited mark in Korea, we find that the cited mark had attained a level of recognition that enabled the general consumers and dealers in Korea to perceive the mark and the goods bearing the mark to be from a specific source at least by June 29, 1996 when the decision to grant registration to the subject registered mark was issued.

(2) The subject registered mark's designated goods, such as umbrella and parasols, are in a different classification of goods than those of the cited mark, apparel. However, they both share the common consumers. It is also quite clear empirically that the trend in the total fashion industry, at least by the time the decision to grant registration to the subject registered mark was issued, was for one company to produce, display and sell apparel, umbrellas and parasols in the same store. We find sufficient cause for consumer confusion in that the use of the subject registered mark on its designated goods would likely be perceived as the use of the owner of the cited mark.

For these reasons, the subject registered mark is likely to confuse or mislead consumers as to the source of the goods with the cited mark, and thus, falls under Article 7(1)(11) of the Trademark Act.

G. Conclusion

Based on the foregoing, the subject registered mark is found to have been registered in violation of Article 7(1)(11) of the Trademark Act. We find the Original Decision that reached a contrary decision to be in error, and we find merit in Plaintiff's claims.

July 19, 2002

Presiding Judge Jinsung Lee

Judge Doo Hyung Lee

Judge Myung Kyu Lee

THE KOREAN BUSINESS FOR A LUXURY BRAND ALMOST DIDN'T HAPPEN

-Luxury Brand JIMMY CHOO-

Are you familiar with the luxury brand Jimmy Choo? In the television drama, "The Time I Loved You," actress Jiwon Ha played the role of Hana Oh, a marketing manager for a shoe company who is extremely meticulous in her work, professionally and personally.

She creates a character who is a cold, metropolitan female whose sophisticated sense of fashion is enhanced by her use of handbags and clutch bags. Her large cross bags effectively match her pencil skirt, doubling her sex appeal. The brown-colored bag that coordinated so well with either the casual or formal look was the Fossil Sydney Workbag. Made especially for today's businesswomen, it can carry documents as well as a 15-inch notebook.

J. Choo Limited looked to undertake trademark registration procedures for its mark, Jimmy Choo, to prepare its Jimmy Choo luxury bag business in Korea. In this process, they retained my services for trademark work. As before, I completed the trademark application process after identifying bags and apparel as its designated goods and was awaiting the results of the examination.

But what a disaster! I had received a Notification for a Response (called Notification of Refusal at the time) that indicated that our mark was not registrable because it was similar to someone else's prior-registered mark for "Patty & Jimmy + device" and that we could file a response, if desired.

My heart felt heavy after receiving this notification. In general, there are two reasons for refusing to register a mark that is considered similar to someone else's prior-registered mark. ▲To prevent another person from using a mark that is similar to one's prior-registered mark allows the mark's owner to protect and maintain the accumulative goodwill in connection with that mark; ▲To avoid confusion among the general consumers as to the source and quality of the products bearing the mark.

Do these two marks actually confuse consumers as to the source and quality? My first impression says "no." But why does my heart still feel heavy?

It was because the Trademark Examination Standard, prior cases from the Intellectual Property Tribunal and even established Supreme Court cases that were relied on as authority at that time all considered two marks to be similar if an element of a mark can be separated from one mark to be used as the mark's abbreviated name and that abbreviated name is similar to the other.

In a way, the examiner's notice of refusal, pursuant to the examination standards and Supreme Court cases, was to be expected, and I felt quite helpless as to how I can overcome the reasons for refusal.

Even if both marks were registered and used, however, I was pretty certain that there would be no consumer confusion as to the source and quality of the goods or that prior-registered mark's reputation would not be damaged. I thus believed that the Trademark Examination Standard and the Supreme Court cases that compelled such marks to always be ruled similar were flawed. I then prepared and sent a report to my U.K. client on the examiner's notification of refusal. I explained the reasons for refusal as follows:

"Based on the Korean Intellectual Property Office's Trademark Examination Standard and established Supreme Court cases, the two marks are deemed similar. For this reason, the chances of overcoming the reasons for refusal are very low. However, I am of the opinion that there should be a reasonable chance of prevailing if we can show that ▲the client's mark, "Jimmy Choo," has never been separated as "Jimmy" and used in that form and ▲the client's mark has always used the mark only in its combined form, "Jimmy Choo."

I added the following opinion to the client:

"Be that as it may, expecting to overcome the refusal at the current examination stage or even Korean Intellectual Property Tribunal level would be unrealistic. Our hope is to have it reversed at the Patent Court or the Supreme Court level where they are relatively free from the mandate of the Examination Standard."

My qualified opinion to the client was then sent.

"Please proceed with the process as we have decided to take your advice and seek reversal of the reasons for refusal. We are forwarding evidentiary materials to show that Jimmy Choo trademark was never used in a separated form of either "Jimmy" or "Choo" and that the mark was always used in its combined form."

Encouraged by my opinion, the client sent their instruction for us to proceed. Thinking this was achievable, I then started to prepare for the written Argument in response to the examiner's notification of refusal. But my office staff was more skeptical.

"This isn't a case where we need to prove that the client's mark is well-known or famous or that the client acquired distinctiveness through use."

I understood their skepticism. This wasn't a case where we need to submit use evidence to defend a "cancellation action for non-use." They were surprised that I took the measure of requesting the client to send as much information and materials on their trademark use as evidence to be used in a case involving the issue of similarity between two marks.

I took particular attention to the fact that the client's mark was never separated into "Jimmy" or "Choo" and used in that form and that it had always been used in its combined form.

"In determining similarity, the mark must be reviewed as "Jimmy Choo" in its entirety, and not separated into "Jimmy" or "Choo" individually. The other party's prior-registered mark, "Patty & Jimmy," likewise is combined with the "&" sign, and as such, it cannot be separated and compared. The two marks must therefore be compared in their entireties, and when this is done, there should be no concern that either mark will be abbreviated into "Jimmy." Likewise, two marks simply have no chance of creating consumer confusion as to the source and quality of the goods."

For this reason, I was confident that the two marks were not similar. I argued that the client's mark must be allowed to be registered, and in so doing, I submitted supporting materials showing the actual use of the client's mark as well as the volume of the use.

I knew that the examiner didn't have discretion to accept my arguments. Despite my arguments, a final refusal was issued. I as well as my client was not too surprised, as we expected it as much.

The examiner could not have defied the Trademark Examination Standard, Intellectual Property Tribunal decisions as well as established Supreme Court cases that held that two marks must be deemed similar if separating the elements of the marks being examined is possible and those elements are identical.

The next step was to file an appeal against the examiner's decision to the Korean Intellectual Property Tribunal. I prepared a written brief using the same line of arguments, further strengthened the evidentiary materials and submitted it. But even the Korean Intellectual Property Tribunal did not have the courage to decide against the Trademark Examination Standard, its prior decisions and the Supreme Court cases. The appeal eventually was dismissed.

We must now take our arguments to the courts without hesitation. In filing my appeal to the Patent Court, I argued that the decision of the Korean Intellectual Property Tribunal was incorrect and that it must be overturned. At least the Patent Court is not bound by the Examination Standard or the decisions of the Korean Intellectual Property Tribunal. Even though there still remain the Supreme Court cases, they are not legally obligated to follow them as those cases are not exactly on point with the case at hand. With heightened hope, I put my heart and soul into the case before the Patent Court. Perhaps my hope for a favorable decision from the Patent Court may have been too ambitious with the overbearing weight of the Supreme Court cases? The Patent Court rendered a decision to dismiss my appeal.

The last bastion of hope was the appeal to the Supreme Court. Because the Supreme Court's review is limited only to the application of law, we could not submit any new evidence. They could only review if there was ▲ insufficient examination by the lower court, which is the Patent Court in this case, ▲ a failure to decide on legal issues, ▲ a misunderstanding of the law relating to similarity of trademarks.

I and the client have now come to the end of the road. How can I persuade these refined, learned and virtuous justices of the Supreme Court to break away from their own precedents and accept my argument? I struggled and struggled again with this dilemma.

So I decided to use, as an example, the name of a law firm that should be familiar to the justices. Even Jesus used numerous metaphors to enlighten the humanity! Would general clients of legal services be confused between Kim & Chang and say, a fictional firm named Chang & Lee, just because they employ the common name of Chang?

Will there be confusion between the law firm name Lee & Ko and a fictional firm called Kim & Lee because of the common name of Lee? How about the law firm of Kim & Chang or the law firm of Lee & Ko and a fictional firm named Kim, Chang, Lee or Ko? Clearly, they would not. Why is that?

Each firm of Kim & Chang and Lee & Ko has long used their respective names in their combined forms, and not separated into any one of Kim, Chang, Lee or Ko. As such, the consumers do not separate them into Kim, Chang, Lee or Ko when perceiving those names. They perceive the name in their entireties, and when separating the names of the law firms into Kim, Chang, Lee or Ko would make it impossible to recognize the identity of any of the firm names.

Likewise, as can be seen from the evidentiary materials on the use of the client's mark submitted to the Patent Court, the client has always used "Jimmy Choo" in that entire form. The consumers also perceive the mark as one entire name. Because there is no reason for the consumers to separate it into "Jimmy" and "Choo", there should be no concern that it would be abbreviated it into just "Jimmy." I explained that there is no confusion with the cited mark "Patty & Jimmy" for these reasons. I guess this explanation was persuasive. The Supreme Court reversed its established case law and remanded the case back for the following reasons:

"Petitioner's trademark, "Jimmy Choo," is not similar to the cited mark, 'Patty & Jimmy,' and as such, we find that the Patent Court, which rendered a decision to the contrary, erred in the application of the law of trademark similarity."

I screamed with delight. The joy I felt in successfully registering my client's trademark "Jimmy Choo" was of course immense, but there was much more pleasure in knowing that my creative argument was able to convince the Supreme Court to reverse their established precedent.

After this Supreme Court case was handed down, there was a significant change from the way the Korean Intellectual Property Office and the courts have uniformly and formally handled prior cases involving trademark similarity. It resulted in the revision of the Korean Intellectual Property Office's Trademark Examination Standard, and this case was featured in the Judicial Research & Training Institute's curriculum as a landmark and model case.

Without this creative best effort, the Korean business for the client's luxury brand "Jimmy Choo" would have been impossible. I am so heartened every time I think about how this type of creative best effort now enables a trademark applicant or someone seeking to use a trademark, which would have been routinely refused registration under the old standard, to now finally acquire trademark registration.

I even received a bonus! Since then, my client for the Jimmy Choo case has shown complete trust in my work. Not only we continue to represent the Jimmy Choo brand, but I continue to work on many other cases that are referred to me by that client.

Korean Supreme Court, August 25, 2006, Decision 2005 Hu 2908.

[Decision of Refusal (Sang)] [Gong September 15, 2006 (258), 1637]

[Issue to Decide]

Whether the subject filed mark "JIMMY CHOO" and prior registered mark ⬚⬚ are similar (passive).

[Gist of Decision]

In reviewing the subject filed mark "JIMMY CHOO" and prior registered mark ⬚⬚, we note that the element of "JIMMY" is common in both marks. However, having considered the weight that this element has in both marks, the extent to which it is combined with other elements, the overall composition of the two marks and where this element is located and the form and concept of both marks, we do not find that general consumers and dealers are likely to be misled or confused as to the source of the designated goods of both marks. We therefore find that the subject filed mark is not similar to the prior registered mark.

[Cited Statute]

Article 7(1)(7) of the Trademark Act

[Cited Cases]

Korean Supreme Court, January 21, 1992, Decision 91 Hu 1359 (Gong 1992, 913) Korean Supreme Court, November 26, 2002, Decision 2001 Hu 3415 (Gong 2003 Sang, 260), Korean Supreme Court, January 10, 2003, Decision 2001 Hu 2986 (Gong 2003 Sang, 650), Korean Supreme Court, February 14, 2003, Decision 2002 Hu 352 (Gong 2003 Sang, 843)

[Full Text]

[Plaintiff, Appellant] Jay Choo (Jersey) Limited (Counsel, Ho Hyun Nahm, Patent Attorney)

[Defendant, Respondent] Commissioner of the Korean Intellectual Property Office

[Original Decision] The Patent Court, September 23, 2005, Decision 2005 Huh 1899

[Order]

The Original Decision is reversed, and the case is remanded to the Patent Court.

[Reasons]

We hereby decide as follows:

1. The Original Decision compared the subject filed mark, JIMMY CHOO, with its designated goods as "trunks, handbags, wallets and umbrellas" and the prior registered marks, including , designated "umbrellas" and "handbags, trunks, non-jewelry wallets." It found that the subject filed mark contains the elements, "JIMMY" and "CHOO"; that its combination does not define a special concept and that the mark's elements are not so intimately connected as to render it unnatural to separate the elements for comparison purposes; as such, that the elements "JIMMY" and "CHOO" can be separated; that the prior-registered marks can similarly be separated into "PATTY" and "JIMMY" elements; that when the subject filed mark and the prior registered marks are separated and compared by the "JIMMY" element common in both marks, the marks are similar in pronunciation and concept so as to conclude that both marks are similar; and therefore, they are likely to mislead or cause confusion among consumers as to the source of the goods when used on their respective designated goods.

2. However, Decision of the Original Decision is Unacceptable

Determination of the similarity of marks is to be made by comparing the appearance, pronunciation and concept objectively, entirely and instinctively in order to assess whether the general consumers would be misled or confused as to the source of goods. Similarity may not be found even if any one of appearance, pronunciation or concept is deemed similar as long as it can be shown that the general consumers are clearly not misled or confused as to the source of the goods based on entirety of the marks. On the other hand, two marks are considered similar if the pronunciation or concept is so similar that general consumers would likely be misled or confused even though there are elements that are dissimilar. (refer to Korean Supreme Court, January 21, 1992, Decision 91 Hu 1359, November 26 2002 Decision 2001 Hu 3415).

Based on the legal principles and records discussed above, the subject filed mark and the cited marks are clearly differentiated in terms of appearance, pronunciation and concept from each other when compared objectively, entirely and instinctively. While the subject filed mark and the cited marks contain the common element of "JIMMY" in their composition, the weight that the JIMMY element has in both marks, the extent to which it is combined with other elements, the overall composition of the two marks and where this element is located and the form and concept of both marks, we do not find that general consumers and dealers are likely to be misled or confused as to the source of the designated goods of the subject filed mark and the cited marks.

Notwithstanding the above, we find that the Original Decision, which concluded that the subject filed mark and the cited marks are similar, erred in misunderstanding the legal principles for trademark similarity or failed to conduct a full review of the case and that the arguments indicated in the reasons for appeal have merit.

3.   Therefore, we hereby reverse the Original Decision and remand this case back to the lower court for a review and decision, and we unanimously decide as provided in the Order.

Chief Justice Ilhwan Park (Presiding Justice)

Yongdam Kim (Coordinating Justice)

Sihwan Park (Justice)

Neunghwan Kim (Justice)

(source: Korean Supreme Court, August 26, 2006, Decision 2005 Hu 2908 [Decision of Refusal (Sang)] General Legal Information Gazette)

TOPPLING THE IMPENETRABLE TOOTHBRUSH DESIGN RIGHT

"We're trying to introduce a new product, but the question of design infringement became a controversial issue internally. Could you please review this situation."

One day, Aekyung Co., Ltd. sought my legal advice prior to the release of their new toothbrush design. I figured that the most important thing to do was to confirm that this does not infringe someone else's rights. At the time I was asked to provide my legal advice, the Korean Intellectual Property Office's information system had not been computerized, and as such, the search for design publications had to be conducted manually. I sent one of my staff to the Korean Intellectual Property Office to conduct the search.

This was not an easy assignment since the voluminous design publications had to be searched by hand. My staff brought back copies of the design publications that were found to have some similarity to the toothbrush design to be released by Aekyung Co., Ltd. I concluded after a careful review that none of those were sufficiently similar to the toothbrush design that our client wanted to release. I then sent a report to the client advising them that I didn't believe that there would be any legal issues with the release of their new toothbrush design.

Soon after this product was released, however, the officer at Aekyung Co., Ltd. who assigned the work to me came to my office with a very frustrated look on his face. I was handed a cease and desist letter. It was a serious cease and desist letter issued in the name of Unilever, a well-known French multinational company, sent through their local counsel which was a major law firm.

"The toothbrush design your company released is similar to the design registration previously acquired by Unilever with the Korean Intellectual Property Office, and it constitutes infringement of their design rights. Immediately stop all manufacturing and sales activities, and pay all damages for your infringement. We will proceed with civil and criminal actions if you do not comply with our demands."

This was the gist of the warning issued by Unilever. After a closer look, our client's released toothbrush design was quite similar to that of Unilever. It truly felt like a helpless situation. The client, our staff, and myself all were dumbfounded.

As for me, the reputation that I had painstakingly built over the years in terms of my specialty and credibility as a patent attorney was at peril. It wasn't only that. I might be responsible for the client's financial losses. But what's going on? A surprise result was awaiting me when I sent my staff back to the Korean Intellectual Property Office to check the records.

"For sure, I can't find the publication for that design."

"That can't be. Check again."

I pressed again, and then, I was told that there were pages "missing." Someone had ripped that page out. Perhaps someone who was conducting a search decided to take the shortcut of cutting the page out rather than making a copy of it. The sky seemed to be falling.

At that point in time, however, the old proverb, "You'll survive even when attacked by a tiger if you keep you cool," came to mind. But surely, as a multinational company, Unilever's registered design will not likely have much weakness.

For a design to be registered, a design must satisfy three conditions: ▲ it must be the first in the world at the time of filing (novelty), ▲ it must not be easily created from an existing design (creativity and inventiveness) and ▲ it must be applicable for mass production (industrial applicability). If any one of these requirements is not met, registration cannot be granted, and if registered despite this deficiency, it would be subject to invalidation.

First, I looked for any weakness in the registration requirements. It was highly unlikely that a global company such as Unilever would copy someone else's design and file it. How can we search a myriad of materials to look for a design that was similar to Unilever's and that was made before theirs? At the time, Internet wasn't as widely used, so this was a monumental task to say the least.

I calmed myself down. I knew that even multinational companies have weak spots. Often times, their marketing team, who is in charge of product releases, and their legal team don't always work side by side. Even if they made the first of its kind in the world, they will lose novelty and will not be able to acquire design registration if the design is advertised, produced, sold or otherwise published prior to the filing of the application. Even if registration is somehow acquired, it becomes subject to invalidation.

I learned that the Korean design registration of Unilever was filed in Korea by claiming "Priority based on Paris Convention." This system allows the applicant to enjoy the same filing date in Korea as their original country of application, in this case France, if they assert their priority within six months from the date they initially filed their design application in France. I figured that we may still prevail if we can find something that shows that the subject design was published prior to their filing date in France.

It is not uncommon for the marketing team, who is eager to release new products, to make advertisements or even sell products without waiting for the legal team to complete their application for design registration. I urgently sent a fax (emails were not in use at the time) to a close friend of mine who worked as a partner in a major intellectual property law firm in France.

"Please conduct a search of any advertisements featuring this design in all French magazines and other media that are regularly used by Unilever for placing their commercial advertisements at or around the time they filed this design in France."

I faxed it out and even called him to confirm. I also asked for an extension of time to respond to Unilever's cease and desist letter. I anxiously awaited for the result.

"We found that Unilever had placed an advertisement in a French magazine for a design that was identical to their Korean design registration prior to their priority filing date."

In less than two weeks, we had received this wonderful news.

I can breathe now. I, the client, and the officer at the client company, all can now escape from this predicament.

Unilever nevertheless moved aggressively, filing for an injunction against manufacture and sale and for a claim for damages from the design infringement. They presumably believed that this design had truly been created by them and that their reliable legal team had built an impenetrable legal protection for this design. In response, we calmly filed an invalidation action against them with the Korean Intellectual Property Tribunal with that French magazine as our evidence. As expected, we prevailed in the invalidation action. By submitting this invalidation decision as evidence in the pending legal actions filed by Unilever, we were able to withstand their barrage of legal assault.

No longer without any obstacles, our client was able to continue to manufacture and sell their toothbrush products. There is always a solution if you have a strong will and creative mind and are able to exert your best efforts. This was truly a memorable case that taught me once again that there is even a way to heaven from hell. It also left many lessons for everyone involved.

For one, the marketing team in any company should always obtain the legal team's clearance before releasing new products. In other words, make sure that all prior reviews are completed as to ▲whether another person's rights are infringed, or ▲whether necessary applications for design, patent or other forms of legal rights and protection have been filed.

There are pretty common instances where miscommunication between the marketing team and the legal team within the corporate structure lead to disastrous results. This is not only isolated to large corporations as even individuals or small companies often are forced to unintentionally donate their valuable intellectual property to the society because they lack the basic knowledge of protecting intellectual property.

This element of "novelty" cannot be more emphasized when it comes to the protection of patent rights, utility model rights and design rights. I will borrow my own words from my book, "Challenging the 21st Century with Intellectual Property Rights," as published by Chosun Ilbo (later adapted into a new book under the title of "Everything Under The Sun Can Be Patented," published by Yega Publishing Company):

* * *

Many times, people only come to think of patents once the product enjoys some success. They seek the advice of patent attorneys with the object of acquiring monopoly rights. In many cases, however, they are too late. The patent application for a newly-developed product must be filed prior to its sale in the market. Otherwise, one will lose the opportunity to acquire a patent permanently. A technology which becomes publicly known before its application is filed is not patentable.

This is also true even if the applicant voluntarily discloses the contents of the invention. Even if a registration were granted in these cases, it would be subject to invalidation. A challenge by a competitor based on this ground will be difficult to defend against. 30 percent or more of those who seek to file patent applications are those who "waive their hands after the bus departs." I continue to feel sorry for those clients who seek to file a patent application for a product, but who also bring with them a product catalogue or advertisement showing the product. In some cases, their products turn out to be quite inventive which generate a lot of excitement in the marketplace.

"We only distributed the catalogues. The products won't be out for a week."

Despite the applicant-candidate's optimism, there are no real solutions.

"Distribution of the catalogues constitutes loss of novelty, and an application for the product will not likely be registered, and even if registered, it will be difficult to exercise the rights. Placing advertisements in newspaper and magazines prior to the filing of the patent application also leads to loss of patentability."

People become dumbfounded when they hear my explanation. In most cases, they had hurried their visit after their acquaintances urged them to "get a patent." In fact, the only "thing" for which they can receive legal protection is the catalogue. Even that is limited to the artistic and creative aspects of the catalogue, which are protected exceptionally as a copyright.

"Our competitors are indiscriminately copying our designs. How can we stop them?"

"Have you started selling your products?"

"Of course. That's why we're looking to obtain a design patent."

"If you're looking to obtain a design patent, you're too late."

It pains me that I have no other way to respond. A person had developed a graceful and luxurious-looking bed, which was enjoying brisk sales. Because it was already advertised, however, it will not qualify for a patent, utility model or design patent. Exceptionally, there is a way to acquire registration in the case of designs if application is filed within 6 months of first publication and in the case of patent and utility models if application is filed within 1 year of first publication.

The most common type of people who visit the offices of patent attorneys is one who is one step too late. We all need to readjust the perception that patents should be considered only after the products are distributed and the initial market response is ascertained.

HYUNDAI MOTOR COMPANY'S "MONG-KOO CHUNG" RECOGNIZED AS A COMMON LAW TRADEMARK

Can a person's name be a trademark? Yes, of course. We often see names of famous fashion designers or sports stars registered as trademarks and used all around us.

But can the name of the chairman of a car company become a trademark? Even in this case, if the name is registered as a trademark, it becomes a mark protected under the trademark law. Even though it may not be the name of a famous star, anyone can register their name as a trademark and use it as a brand.

Then, can a name not be registered as a trademark, but still receive protection as a trademark? Yes, again. For example, an unregistered name of a famous fashion designer can receive protection under the "Unfair Competition Prevention and Trade Secret Protection Act" if that name has been used on products as a result of which the name has become well-known among the general consumers. Would the unregistered name of the chairman of a car company still be protected as a trademark?

An individual in the U.S. obtained a domain name registration for "chungmongku.com" and "chungmongku.net", which is the same name as the Chairman Mong-Koo Chung of Hyundai Motor Company. The same person opened a website using the same domain name and were selectively uploading negative articles on Hyundai Motor Company, Chairman Chung's family and Chairman Chung himself as to rub salt into the wound.

He appeared to have had an ulterior motive of sitting on the domain name registration and then seeking compensation for its transfer. We considered it as a typical blueprint for cybersquatters. There are ways to deal with cybersquatters. Without offering any payment to them, we can seek cancellation or compel transfer of the domain name registration.

Most global companies prefer to take the path of resolving cybersquatting issues by legal action over settlement payment even where the costs of the legal action are much more than the financial compensation sought by the cybersquatters. As such, cybersquatters have begun to realize that there isn't much benefit coming to them by registering and occupying domain names using someone else's name or company name, and consequently, there has been a significant reduction of such cybersquatters.

Because of the nature of the domain names, such as ▲its uniqueness anywhere in the world, ▲global use without border, ▲conflict with the territoriality principle of intellectual property and ▲enforceability of decisions, there is a limitation to how much judicial intervention and resolution can play a role. As such, there is an urgent demand for resolution of disputes in this regard that is inexpensive, speedy and valid.

In this regard, ICANN, the institution responsible for coordinating the maintenance and procedure for domain names, has adopted Uniform Domain Name Dispute Resolution Policy (UDRP).

***

I was retained to represent Hyundai Motor Company and its Chairman Mong-Koo Chung in a domain name dispute case involving "chungmonku. com" and "chungmongku.net."

I recommended to the clients that a complaint should be filed before the World Intellectual Property Organization pursuant to the UDRP procedure. The language used for this procedure was English, the language used in the registration agreement. But there were many hills to climb.

In order to cancel the domain name registration or receive a transfer of the same under the UDRP procedure, the petitioner must argue and prove three elements:

▲First, the subject domain name must be identical or confusingly similar to certain unregistered common law and registered trademarks and service marks, ▲Second, the owner of the subject domain name registration has no rights or legitimate interests in the domain names, and ▲Third, the domain names have been registered and subsequently used in bad faith.

The problem was the first element - whether Chairman Chung's name was a trademark. They had never registered this name anywhere in the world, including Korea. They certainly never produced and sold cars bearing his name as a brand like a famous fashion designer.

After much thought, I came up with the argument of a service mark concept. I focused on the fact that the name "Mong-Koo Chung" would readily conjure up the auto industry in Korea and elsewhere even though the name of Hyundai Motor Company's Chairman was not actually used as a brand for cars.

I collected evidence supporting the multitude of contributions and activities of Chairman Chung in the auto industry as well. I also emphasized the numerous awards he received from a variety of organizations around the world for his contributions to the auto industry. The success story of Chairman Chung as the engine behind the legend of Hyundai Motor Company was also weaved into my arguments. I argued that "Hyundai Motors = Chairman Mong-Koo Chung," and as such, that "Mong-Koo Chung" was a common-law trademark symbolizing the auto-related services provided by Hyundai Motor Company. It was not too difficult to argue and establish the other two elements.

I put out my best efforts, and I held my breath to await the WIPO's decision. What made this more dramatic was that we were dealing with the name of the chairman of a car company, and not the name of a famous fashion designer or a sports star. Moreover, we were arguing that this name, which hadn't been registered as a trademark anywhere in the world, should be deemed a common law service mark. No one could deny that this was a creative approach.

Then, a heart-pounding decision came down. I became more ecstatic as I began reading through the long decision. The panel reviewing this case pointed out that "the Complainants' representatives have presented a meticulous case," a recognition not commonly used by the panels in these types of cases.

"For these reasons, the Complainants have common law trademark rights in the name Chung Mong Koo and both domain names are confusingly similar to that name."

They had recognized that we had satisfied the requirements for the first element. As a result of this decision, we were able to receive assignment of the relevant domain names without paying anything to the domain name registrant. This case again is a reminder of how great results can be achieved by developing an unprecedented but a creative idea and putting out your best efforts.

WIPO Arbitration and Mediation Center
ADMINISTRATIVE PANEL DECISION

Chung, Mong Koo and Hyundai Motor Company v. Individual
Case No. D2005-1068

The Parties

The Complainants are Chung, Mong Koo, Seoul, Republic of Korea and Hyundai Motor Company, Seoul, Republic of Korea, represented by H.H. Nahm International Patent & Law Firm (author's note: former name of BARUN IP & LAW), Republic of Korea.

The Respondent is Individual, Totowa, New Jersey, U.S.A.

2. The Domain Names and Registrar

The disputed domain names <chungmongku.com> and <chungmongku. net> are registered with Network Solutions, LLC.

3. Procedural History

The Complaint was filed with the WIPO Arbitration and Mediation Center (the "Center") on October 10, 2005. On October 10, 2005, the Center transmitted by email to Network Solutions, LLC a request for registrar verification in connection with each of the domain names at issue. On October 13, 2005, Network Solutions, LLC transmitted by email to the Center its verification response confirming that the Respondent in each case is listed as the registrant and providing the contact details for the administrative, billing, and technical contact. In response to a notification by the Center that the Complaint was administratively deficient, the Complainants filed an amendment to the Complaint on October 21, 2005. The Center verified that the Complaint together with the amendment to the Complaint satisfied the formal requirements of the Uniform Domain Name Dispute Resolution Policy (the "Policy"), the Rules for Uniform Domain Name Dispute Resolution Policy (the "Rules"), and the WIPO Supplemental Rules for Uniform Domain Name Dispute Resolution Policy (the "Supplemental Rules").

In accordance with the Rules, paragraphs 2(a) and 4(a), the Center formally notified the Respondent of the Complaint, and the proceedings commenced on November 2, 2005. In accordance with the Rules, paragraph 5(a), the due date for Response was November 22, 2005. The Respondent did not submit any response. Accordingly, the Center notified the Respondent's default on November 28, 2005.

The Center appointed The Honourable Neil Anthony Brown QC as the sole panelist in this matter on December 12, 2005. The Panel finds that it was properly constituted. The Panel has submitted the Statement of Acceptance and Declaration of Impartiality and Independence, as required by the Center to ensure compliance with the Rules, paragraph 7.

The language of the Registration Agreement in the case of each domain name is English and, accordingly, pursuant to paragraph 11 of the Rules the language of the administrative proceeding is English.

4. Factual Background

The First Complainant is the Chairman and Chief Executive Officer of the Second Complainant which was founded in 1967 and which is part of the very large Hyundai automotive Group.

The Second Complainant is the registered owner of a large number of international trade and service marks, including one in particular which is HYUNDAI and which was registered as a Korean trademark on September 6, 1989. It also has trademark and service marks for HYUNDAI, HMC HYUNDAI and a well-known 'H device' in most countries of the world. However, the proceeding is also concerned with the claim of both Complainants that they both have a common law trademark and service mark rights in the personal name of the First Complainant, CHUNG MONG KOO.

The Respondent registered the two domain names in question on February 9, 1999.

5. Parties' Contentions

A. Complainant

The Complainants allege that the contentious domain names <chungmongku.com> and <chungmongku.net> should no longer be registered in the name of the Respondent but that they should be transferred to one or other of the Complainants.

They contend that this should be done because, within the meaning of paragraph 4 the Policy, the domain names are identical or confusingly similar to certain unregistered common law and registered trademarks and service marks, the Respondent has no rights or legitimate interests in the domain names and the domain names have been registered and subsequently used in bad faith. The Complainants maintain that they can prove all three of these requirements and that the appropriate remedy is to transfer the domain names, preferably to the Second Complainant, but alternatively to the First Complainant.

In support of its case on the first of these three elements, the Complainants maintain that the domain names <chungmongku.com> and <chungmongku.net> are confusingly similar to the unregistered trademark and service marks CHUNG MONG KOO, which is the personal name of the Chairman and Chief Executive Officer of the Second Complainant. The Complainants say that they both have rights in this trademark and service mark. They point to the obvious similarity between the two expressions as they appear in the domain names and Mr. Chung's actual name and also to the likelihood of confusion between them. They also maintain that the name of the First Complainant is very prominent and that he is identified with the Second Complainant and generally with the Hyundai Group. Indeed, they say, the Respondent chose Mr. Chung's name for the domain names deliberately, so as to attract unsuspecting members of the public whom the Respondent would then subject to very damaging and abusive criticisms of Mr. Chung and Hyundai.

The Complainants also rely on a series of registered trademarks and service marks which are owned by the Second Complainant and which are in HYUNDAI, HMC HYUNDAI and 'H device.'

The Complainants then contend, to establish the second element, that the same conduct as that already described shows that the Respondent does not and cannot have any rights or legitimate interests in the domain names, for his or her use of them is entirely illegitimate. In particular, the Complainants say that the Respondent has no rights or interests in the domain names because he or she does not conduct a business under that names, is not commonly known by it and does not use it in connection with a bona fide offering of goods and services.

Finally, the Complainants allege that the domain names were registered and are being used in bad faith. The Complainants contend that this is so because the Respondent chose the name so that he or she could deceptively attract consumers to his website and that constitutes bad faith. Moreover, they maintain that the Respondent cannot claim he is operating some sort of valid criticism site, for the Respondent is anonymous, the domain names falsely give the impression that they are genuine sites for Hyundai and Mr. Chung and they give no clue that they are actually being used for some very abusive criticism of both Hyundai and Mr. Chung.

B. Respondent

The Respondent did not reply to the Complainants' contentions.

6. Discussion and Findings

Paragraph 15 of the Rules provides that the Panel is to decide the complaint on the basis of the statements and documents submitted and in accordance with the Policy, the Rules and any rules and principles of law that it deems applicable.

It is appropriate therefore to note the fact that the Respondent has not made a Response to the Complaint does not avoid the necessity of examining the issues and of doing so in the light of the evidence. In fact, Paragraph 4 of the Policy expressly provides that in administrative proceedings '...the complainant bears the onus of proof' and it follows that, as the proceeding is a civil one, the standard of proof must be the balance of probabilities. The onus of proof clearly remains on the Complainants even where, as in the present case, the Respondent has not made a Response or put in a submission. That principle has been enunciated on many occasions by UDRP panels.

The Complainants must therefore establish all three of the elements specified in Paragraph 4(a) of the Policy on the balance of probabilities before an order can be made to transfer the domain names.

However, in the course of deciding whether that onus has been discharged, it is possible to draw inferences both from the evidence that has been submitted and, in appropriate cases, from silence. Indeed, Paragraph 14 of the Rules specifically provides that if a Party does not comply with its obligations, the Panel is still required to proceed to a decision, but it is also required to draw such inferences 'as it considers appropriate' from the non-compliance.

That being so, the Panel will now proceed to enquire if the Complainants have discharged the onus on them to prove each of the three elements specified in paragraph 4(a) of the Policy.

Those three elements, all of which must be proved, are:

A. That the Respondent's domain names are identical or confusingly similar to a name, trademark or service mark in which the Complainants have rights; and

B. That the Respondent has no rights or legitimate interests in respect of the domain names; and

C. That the domain names have been registered or subsequently used in bad faith.

The Panel will deal with each of these requirements in turn.

A. Identical or Confusingly Similar

The Complainants contend that the two domain names are confusingly similar to a common law trademark and service mark that the First Complainant has in his own name. It is clear that <chungmongku.com> and <chungmongku.net> are both similar to the name Chung Mong Koo; the only differences are that the constituent personal names all commence with a capital letter, that the 'Koo' of the second given name is spelt 'ku' in the domain names and that the domain names carry the addition of two of the generic Top Level Domain suffixes, '.com' and '.net' respectively. These variations do not detract from the otherwise confusing similarity between the domain names and the claimed trademark and service mark, as the capital letters would not be used in a domain name, the spelling of the name as 'ku' is apparently understood in the Korean language to be the equivalent of 'Koo' and the gTLD suffixes have never been taken to detract from what would otherwise amount to confusing similarity.

Moreover, the domain names have the appearance of being virtually the same as Mr. Chung's name and the unchallenged evidence is that they are also pronounced in the same way as Mr. Chung's name. Finally, there is nothing in the evidence and nothing submitted by the Respondent to show that the domain names are anything other than confusingly similar to the common law trademark and service marks that are claimed.

However, the more substantial and difficult issue is whether the personal name of the First Complainant is in fact an unregistered trademark or service mark as is contended for by both Complainants. To succeed, the Complainants have to show that they, or at least one of them, has an interest in a trademark or service reflecting the personal name Chung Mong Koo.

This question raises the contentious issue of whether a personal name that has not been registered as a trademark can ever constitute a common law trademark. The issue is contentious enough for it to be the subject of a series of UDRP decisions and an issue discussed in the valuable WIPO Overview of WIPO Panel Views on Selected UDRP Questions.

However: The name in question should be actually used in trade or commerce to establish unregistered trademark rights. Merely having a famous name (such as a businessman, or religious leader) is not necessarily sufficient to show unregistered trademark rights.

The Complainants also rely on Philip Berber v. Karl Flanagan and KP Enterprises, WIPO Case No. D2000-0661 and Steven Rattner v. BuyThisDomainName (JohnPepin), WIPO Case No. D2000-0402, which are to the same effect.

In the present case, the Complainants' representatives have presented a meticulous case, involving the history of the company and the involvement of the First Complainant in all of its activities. The uncontradicted evidence is that he has been internationally recognized as a leading figure in the automotive industry and that the awards showered on him have not simply been because of his involvement in that industry in general, but because it has been solely with the Hyundai Group. For example, when Mr. Chung was inducted into the US Automotive Hall of Fame, the Chairman of that institution observed that the recipient was …recognized as a world-class automotive expert, 27 years after he first entered the automobile sector as the president of Hyundai Service in 1974.

It is not necessary to recite the evidence set out in a series of exhibits annexed to the Complaint other than to say that it establishes the First Complainant's fame and achievement, that these qualities have been recognized internationally, that they are on the public record and widely reported in the trade and general media and, most importantly, that they are at all times linked with the Hyundai Group and its success. Indeed, the record is clear that Mr. Chung is personally recognized as having restored the Group's fortunes to the point where its present success is largely due to him, that he has given it a reputation for quality control because of his own personal pre-occupation with that objective and that there is a widely held view that the company's fortunes would suffer if he were not in charge of them. The evidence and the public record show that Mr. Chung has put his personal imprimatur on the company and that the company is now virtually identified with him. In this particular case (which will not be the same in all other cases concerned with this issue,) the identification of the person with the company is strengthened by the fact that Mr. Chung is a substantial owner of the company, his family name has long been associated with it, as in the Monty and Pat Roberts, Inc case(supra) and a Google search reveals 48,000 references to him.

Accordingly, the Panel concludes that the First Complainant's name is being used for trade or commerce, that this is being done for the benefit of both Complainants and that within the principle in Rattner's Case, both Complainants have an interest in protecting his name for commercial use, for it materially advances the fortunes of both the company and the First Complainant himself if he is pre-eminent in its affairs.

This conclusion is reinforced by the inference that the Respondent must have been of the same opinion when he registered the domain names. He registered both domain names using Mr. Chung's name. He did not register them using Hyundai's name. The only inference open is that he did this because he knew that people looking for a website on Hyundai were just as likely to look for it under Mr. Chung's name as under Hyundai's name. Indeed, having registered two domain names under Mr. Chung's name and none under Hyundai's name, he must be taken to have believed that people were more likely to look for Hyundai under Mr. Chung's name than under Hyundai's name.

Moreover, the Respondent can hardly be heard to say that the Complainants do not have a commercial interest in Mr. Chung's name when he took aim at Hyundai by registering two domain names in Mr. Chung's name.

It should also be pointed out that the Second Complainant has registered more than twenty domain names in various combinations of the spelling of Mr. Chung's name, for the commercial reality is that people seeking information on Hyundai will seek out Mr. Chung's name.

As in the Monty Roberts Case, the Respondent has also directed the use of the name '...precisely at the market for Complainant's services...', being in the present case potential buyers of Hyundai motor vehicles.

For these reasons, the Complainants have common law trademark rights in the name Chung Mong Koo and both domain names are confusingly similar to that name.

The Complainants have therefore satisfied the first requirement.

B. Rights or Legitimate Interests

The Panel's task in deciding if a registrant has any rights or legitimate interests in a domain name is made more difficult when the registrant is in default and does not make a Response or any other form of submission.

That is so in the present case, where the Respondent was given notice on November 2, 2005 that the administrative proceeding had been commenced and was served with a copy of the Complaint, which of course included the allegation that he had no rights or legitimate interests in the domain names <chungmongku.com> and <chungmongku.net>.

The Respondent was also given notice that he had until November 22, 2005 to send in his Response, that he would be in default if he did not do so and that, by virtue of Paragraph 14 of the Rules, the Panel might draw appropriate inferences from that default.

As the Respondent is in default, the Panel, after considering all of the evidence, draws the inference that the Respondent has no rights or legitimate interests in the domain names. It is appropriate to draw that inference because, first, if the Respondent had any such rights or interests, it was a simple matter to say what they were. Moreover, the substance of what has happened in this matter is that the Respondent has taken the First Complainant's personal name, giving rise to the possible explanation that he did so for some deceptive purpose, an inference which is easy to draw against someone who takes another's name without consent. If there were, however, a more innocent or legitimate explanation for his conduct, which of course is also possible, the Respondent could have given it, but this he has failed to do. The inference that the Respondent took the First Complainant's name for an illegitimate purpose is reinforced by the fact that the Respondent has sought to hide behind a cloak of anonymity in registering the domain names in the name 'Individual'.

In the absence of an innocent explanation for all of this conduct, as the Panel observed in Pharmacia & Upjohn AB v. Dario H. Romero, WIPO Case No. D2000-1273, the Panel is entitled to draw inferences adverse to the

Respondent's interests on that issue and to assume that 'any evidence of the Respondent would not have been in his favour'.

Furthermore, the Respondent had the opportunity to bring himself within paragraph 4(c) of the Policy which sets out several criteria, any one of which, if proved, 'is to be taken to demonstrate' the registrant's rights or legitimate interests in the domain name.

However, the Respondent has not endeavored to establish even one of the criteria set out in Paragraph 4(c) of the Policy, giving rise to the inevitable inference that he could not do so by credible evidence.

Finally, even on the most charitable interpretation of the website to which the contentious domain names resolve, the Panel is not prepared to find that the Respondent could bring him or herself within any of these criteria.

Nor could the Respondent remotely succeed in arguing that he had the protection of free speech or that this was one of the so-called protest cases. That is so for the reason that the Respondent has not been open or transparent and has not publicly announced that his domain names will lead to a criticism or protest site. Instead, he has falsely pretended that the domain names will lead to genuine websites for Mr. Chung and Hyundai. See in this regard: Delta Air Transport NV (trading as SN Brussels Airlines) v. Theodule De Souza, WIPO Case No. D2003-0372; Hollenbeck Youth Center, Inc. v. Stephen Rowland, WIPO Case No. D2004-0032; Banque Cantonale de Geneve v. Primatex Group S.A., WIPO Case No. D2001-0477; and Triodos Bank NV v. Ashley Dobbs, WIPO Case No. D2002-0776.

The anonymity of the Respondent adds to the impossibility of a finding that he had rights or legitimate interests of this sort.

The Complainants have therefore made out their case on the second requirement.

C. Registered and Used in Bad Faith

Paragraph 4(b) of the Policy lists a number of circumstances which, without limitation, are deemed to be evidence of the registration and use of a domain name in bad faith. Those circumstances are:

(i) circumstances indicating that [the respondent has] registered or acquired the domain name primarily for the purpose of selling, renting, or otherwise transferring the domain name registration to the complainant who is the owner of the trademark or service mark or to a competitor of that complainant, for valuable consideration in excess of [the respondent's] documented out-of-pocket costs directly related to the domain name; or

(ii) [the respondent has] registered the domain name in order to prevent the owner of the trademark or service mark from reflecting the mark in a corresponding domain name, provided that [the respondent has] engaged in a pattern of such conduct; or

(iii) [the respondent has] registered the domain name primarily for the purpose of disrupting the business of a competitor; or

(iv) by using the domain name, [the respondent has] intentionally attempted to attract, for commercial gain, Internet users to [the respondent's] website or other on-line location, by creating a likelihood of confusion with the complainant's mark as to the source, sponsorship, affiliation, or endorsement of [the respondent's] website or location or of a product or service on [the respondent's] website or location.

The Panel accepts the persuasive arguments advanced in the Complaint to the effect that the known conduct of the Respondent in registering the domain names and using them to direct internet traffic to a website 'definitely constitutes bad faith as stipulated under paragraph 4(b)(iii) and (iv) of the Policy'. The English translation of pages of the website that are annexed to the Complaint have given the Panel a clear picture of its contents. In essence it is a website which purports to be the website of Hyundai and Mr. Chung Mong Koo, for it is reached by domain names consisting solely of his name, it includes a series of questions where the answers are by implication being given by Mr. Chung, it carries a photograph of Mr. Chung with greetings from the website and it gives his name in Chinese characters. It also underlines the connection between Mr. Chung and the Second Complainant by prominently displaying the word HYUNDAI which is a registered Korean and international trademark and by inviting the reader to send an email to chungmongku@[email address]. The real vice in the website is that it poses questions, the answers to which are derogatory of Hyundai and which are falsely portrayed as coming by implication from Mr. Chung himself. Whilst this is being done, the website carries the exhortation 'don't buy Hyundai', an assertion that the First Complainant illegally paid 9 billion won to a political party and another assertion that Hyundai is 'junk'. Clearly some consumers will find all of this ludicrous and will ignore it. But the Panel finds that in all probability at least some people will take notice of the false assertions on the website and many more will certainly be misled and confused by them, leaving an overall impression that is damaging to both Complainants, derogatory of them and disruptive of the Second Complainant's business and the First Complainant's management of it.

That conduct comes within paragraph 4(b)(iii) of the Policy, for, although it is unlikely that this process was devised by a competitor in the automotive industry, its perpetrators are certainly competing with both Complainants in the official presentation of the Hyundai case and the information market about its products.

In any event, the same conduct comes within paragraph 4(b)(iv) of the Policy, for it is intentional conduct designed to create confusion as to whether the website and the assertions carried on it are genuine products and services of Hyundai and Mr. Chung.

As to whether this is conduct engaged in for 'commercial gain' the Panel accepts that there is a probability of that being the intention, either in the benefits to a competitor if Hyundai's business suffers from the deception or, more likely, the establishment of a track record in using the domain names and attracting 'hits', that can then be turned to a commercial advantage later or alternatively being able to build up a list of visitors to the site.

Moreover, the deceptive nature of the entire modus operandi of a registrant supplying false information to hide his identity is itself evidence of bad faith: Telstra Corporation v. Nuclear Marshmallows, WIPO Case No. D2000-0003.

Finally, as has already been said under paragraph 4(a)(ii) of the Policy, any attempt to make out a case that this was a legitimate 'protest' site, relying on free speech to negate any finding a bad faith would fail. That is so because of the inherent deception that is at the root of the way the site has been constructed. It is one thing to criticize Hyundai, even unfairly, but it is another thing altogether to mislead people into believing that it is the Chairman and CEO of a company who has taken to disparaging it.

The Complainants have therefore succeeded in proving this element.

7. Decision

As the Complainants have made out all of the elements necessary, the Panel is of the view that the domain names should be transferred from the Respondent. The Complainants say that their first preference is that the domain names be transferred to the Second Complainant. However, they also say that if the panel 'deems more appropriate', it requests that the domain names be transferred to the First Complainant.

The Complainants' case was that both Complainants had interests in the common law trademark and service mark in Mr. Chung's name and the Panel has so decided. They both therefore have an entitlement to the domain names.

However, courts and tribunals called upon to make orders of this sort traditionally take into account the balance of convenience and all the circumstances. The Panel will therefore order that the domain names be transferred to the Second Complainant, specifically for the following reasons. First, although the trademark and service mark embody Mr. Chung's name, it is because of his association with the company that it is a trademark and service mark at all, so the link with the company is of paramount importance. Secondly, the Second Complainant already has a series of domain names in various spellings of Mr. Chung's name and it seems convenient that all relevant domain names should be in the one ownership. Thirdly, if the Panel orders that the domain name be transferred to Mr. Chung, he will no doubt transfer it to the company as a matter of practicality, so that step may as well be taken immediately as a matter of convenience.

This course also seems consistent with The Chase Manhattan Corporation and Robert Fleming Holdings Limited v. Paul Jones, WIPO Case No. D2000-0731, where the order was made after agreement between two Complainants and Boston Beer Corporation and BBC Brands, LLC v. Netsolutions Proxy Services, WIPO Case No. D2004-0920, where the order was for transfer to the Complainants 'or as they may direct'.

For all the foregoing reasons, in accordance with paragraphs 4(i) of the Policy and 15 of the Rules, the Panel orders that the domain names, <chungmongku.com> and <chungmongku.net> be transferred to the Second Complainant.

The Honourable Neil Anthony Brown QC
Sole Panelist
Dated: December 21, 2005

EPILOGUE

ENJOYING LONGEVITY - LIVING TO 120

Those who waste their time are not qualified to complain that life is too short. Life is time, and time is life. Some just loaf through life, take naps for no good reason or just sleep in all day. They do things distracted and without focus and thus are inefficient, squandering away precious time. They are in effect stealing time from themselves, their employers or anyone they come across.

"You use 24 hours like they're 72. You work hard, write all the books and articles you want, take numerous overseas business trips, attend all kinds of seminars, play golf, are loyal to your family… when do you have time for all that?

Few of my friends often tell me.

"Don't worry. I get all the sleep I need."

I respond nonchalantly. But my life has been intimately marked with passion. As a husband to a woman and a father of two children, I prepared for and passed the grueling patent attorney examination while working for a company. I take back seat to no one, other than airline crew members, when it comes to accumulating flight mileage.

This will be my 8th book. Having written almost 400 decisions on domain name disputes that make up about 40 books at 300 page per book, I could probably publish a grand series of books on this topic. I guess my friends were right when I think about my constant activities, like trying to master Japanese, continuously writing books and presenting papers, and always balancing work and family.

I did some calculations, assuming that I'm spending 72 hours in a 24-hour day. Suppose that I spent my life like everyone else until I was 30. In that 30 some years since I was 30 where I lived 3 times more than others, I could say that I have lived 120 years. And not that I am so old that I am unable to stay active - I am still enjoying a healthy and spirited 120 years of longevity.

Frankly, I have no regrets. Born to this beautiful world, I have lived well and in good health, and I have accomplished a lot. I can depart this world with joy and without regret. So when I eventually return to where I came from, no one should be saddened.

What is the secret to a 120-year centenarian? It's certainly not taking wild ginseng or antlers. It is about "setting priorities" and "focusing on where I am today." In other words, it's "choice and focus." Of course, if someone asked me whether I lived my life to its fullest 100% immaculate way, the correct answer would be no. I did not and could not live a perfect life. But I can say this. You can achieve all that you want if you prioritize and pursue each of them. While you may not be able to get to some things that are down on the list, they are likely to be mostly not very important anyway.

Focus is especially critical. When meeting someone, focus on the eyes and mouth of the person in front of you, and don't get distracted. When eating, enjoy the meal with as much joy as you can summon. When working, don't get up to turn on the TV or fiddle with the cell phone until you are finished with the task. When reading, imagine sitting across the table with the author. When praying, trust that God is next to you. And when you are sleeping, imagine yourself dead so all the worldly concerns can stop in their tracks.

Work hard, but don't do it without thinking and planning. Is there another way? Is there a new approach? Can I create my own unique solution? Is there a more effective alternative? Think and think again while working. In other words, give it your creative best effort.

"I am not simply one of 7 billion people. My own unique existence was created in a truly precious time and space. There will never be anything resembling me before and after. I tell my children whenever I can.

"Look at the pebbles on the bank of the river. Each of them looks different. Why are you not as round as me? Why are you triangular? Why are you oblong? Don't complicate things by thinking too much. Take things for what they are. Each of us is different. Because we are all different, there is value in each and every one of us.

We follow and benefit from so many things that have been created in the course of mankind, and each one of us has a unique, dazzling formula for life. For this very reason, "I" have a precious and treasured existence. Likewise, we must acknowledge and respect each and every "you" and "them." Each and every one as the world's most unique existence."

You must live with creative best effort. Your life will be filled with joy when you can shine "your own unique, dazzling light." I am certain that your own "light" will contribute to the mankind in its own way. According to the profound will of God, I mean. "Me" writing this book today, while hospitalized, is the unique work that only "I" can engage in. This is the creative best effort with which God has blessed me.

ABOUT THE AUTHOR

■   QUALIFICATIONS·PROFESSIONAL   EXPERIENCE   IN
INTELLECTUAL PROPERTY

Passed the 23rd patent attorney examination and licensed as patent
attorney in 1986. Worked 30 years as Partner at Central International Patent
and Law Firm and as Lead Partner at BARUN IP & LAW Firm.

Acquired extensive experience through variety of cases in the areas of
registration, opposition, cancellation actions, invalidation actions, scope
confirmation trials, litigation and appeals in connection with trademarks,
designs and patents as well as international licensing of trademarks and related
intellectual property.

■ ACTIVITIES - KOREA AND INTERNATIONAL

● Advisory Member, Presidential Advisory Council on Science &
Technology, a Constitutional institution serving as an advisory board to the
President of the Republic of Korea (2005-2006)

● President, Korea Chapter, Asia Patent Attorneys Association (APAA)
(2012-2015)

● President, Korea Trademark Society (1999-2000)

● Chairman, Korean Internet Address Dispute Resolution Committee
(2014 - 2016); Chairman of APAA Trademark Committee (2003-2009),
Current Coordinator, National Group Presidents' Meeting of APAA

(2015-present); Current Vice President of Intellectual Property Forum under Korean National Congress (2016-present); Current Panelist on U.S. National Arbitration Forum (NAF),, World Intellectual Property Organization (WIPO), Asian Domain Name Dispute Resolution Centre (ADNDRC), and Czech Arbitration Court (CAC); Panelist of Korean Internet Address Dispute Resolution Committee (2002-2016)

● Current Arbitrator or Panelist on Hong Kong International Arbitration Centre (HKIAC), Korean Commercial Arbitration Board.

● Member, Korean Industrial Property Law Association, Intellectual Property Forum, International Trademark Association (INTA), European Communities Trademark Association (ECTA), Pharmaceutical Trademarks Group (PTMG), the Association Internationale pour la Protection de la Propriete (AIPPI)

● Director and Member, Korean Chapter of Federation Internationale Des Conseils En Propriete Intellectuelle (FICPI)

● Director of International Affairs (March 2000-February 2002) and Member, Korean Patent Attorneys Association

■AWARDS

● Selected as one of 'The World's Leading Experts in Trademark Law' in 1996 by 'Euromoney Publications PLC' based in London

● Selected as "Leading Intellectual Property Lawyers in Asia Pacific," "Most Highly Acclaimed Legal Experts in the Intellectual Property Practical Area(s)," "Highly recommended Asia-Pacific focused Lawyers in the Intellectual Property Area(s)" for 7 straight years (2007-2013), by 'Asia Law'

● Recognized as the 'Man of the Year in Law 2010' by American Biographical Institute (ABI).

● Awarded as the "Winner of the 2010 New Quality Innovation Award (Service Innovation)" for the first time by a professional in the field of patents and legal services in Korea

• Awarded "Award in Writing" from the Korean Academy of Invention Education (2015)

■BROADCASTING·PUBLISHED ARTICLES·BOOKS

• Host of Maeil Business News TV (MBN)'s Weekly Program, "Ho-Hyun Nahm's Interesting Patent Stories"

• Author, "Challenging the 21st Century with Intellectual Property Rights", selected as a best seller in the area of Politics and Business Management (published by Chosun Daily Newspaper)

• Published "Challenging the 21st Century with Intellectual Property Rights" in English and Japanese

• Author, "Everything Under the Sun can be Patented," (Yega Publishing Co.)

• Author, "Change Your Life with Ideas" (Park Young Books)

• Co - Author, "From Edison to iPod" (2010) (Business Map)

• Contributor, Korean Chapter of **INTA** International Trademark Association the International Opposition Guide (http://www.inta.org/Oppositions/Pages/IOG.aspx)

• Contributor, Korean Chapter of **INTA** International Trademark Association Enforcement _ An International Litigation Guide (http://www.inta.org/EnforcementGuides/

Pages/EnforcementGuides.aspx)

• Contributor, Korean Chapter of Doman Name Law and Practice - An International Handbook, Second Edition (English version 2015, Oxford University Press)

■LECTURES (KOREA AND INTERNATIONAL)·RESEARCH ·PAPERS

• Lectures presented at the international meetings at AIPPI, INTA, FICPI, PTMG.

• Lecturer, Sookmyung Women's University (2000)

• Lecturer in Intellectual Property, Korean National Police University (2011), Seoul National University, CIPO Executive Intellectual Property Program (2013), International Management Institute of the Federation of Korean Industries (2000 - Present), Korean Bar Association, The Korean Constitutional Court, Ministry of the Interior

■ SPEAKING ENGAGEMENTS·PRESENTATIONS

① Time / ② Subject / ③ Location / ④ Publication / ⑤ Language Used

----

① May 2015 ② Update on Domain Name Dispute Resolutions including New gTLDs ③ Seoul, Korea ④ ECCK Legal Seminar ⑤ English

----

① Feb 2015 ② New Aspects of Resolving Disputes Involving New gTLD and Domain Names ③ Seoul, Korea ④ Intellectual Property Forum ⑤ Korean

----

① Oct 2014 ② Ensuring Internet Security, Domain Name and Trademark Protection ③ Seoul, Korea ④ ALB Korea Conference ⑤ English

----

① Apr 2014 ② Protection of Non-Traditional Trademarks in Korea ③ Kyoto, Japan ④ FICPI Kyoto Symposium ⑤ English

----

① Mar 2014 ② Trademark Dispute Cases and Litigation Strategies ③ Seoul, Korea ④ Seoul National University IP Dispute Strategies and Business Specialists Training Program ⑤ Korean

----

① Jan 2014 ② How Does UDRP Affect the Evolution of cc TLD Dispute Resolution Policies - Perspectives from .kr ③ Kuala Lumpur, Malaysia
④ 2014 ADNDRC Conference ⑤ English

----

① Oct 2013 ② Are Goods and Services Specifications Inflation Proof - Perspective of South Korea ③ Sorrento, Italy ④ 14th FICPI Open Forum ⑤ English

----

① Jun 2013 ② Company Brands and Strategies and Cases Involving Trademark Protection ③ Seoul, Korea ④ Seoul National University, CIPO Executive Intellectual Property Management Program ⑤ Korean

----

① Feb 2012 ② Best Strategies to Acquire and Utilize Knowledge Capital in Korea - Under Newly Developed IP Law System - ③ Ahmadabad, India ④ 8th Annual International Seminar of markPatent.org ⑤ English

----

① Dec 2011 ② Counterfeiting and Criminal Sanctions in Korea ③ Seoul, Korea ④ FICPI Korea Symposium ⑤ English

----

① Nov 2011 ② Report on WIPO Panelist Meeting and WIPO Advanced Workshop on Domain Name Dispute Resolution ③ Seoul, Korea ④ Internet Address Dispute Resolution Council Workshop ⑤ Korean

----

① Sept 2011 ② Strategies for Utilizing Intellectual Property for a Successful Corporate Management ③ Seoul, Korea ④ 21st Century Business Forum ⑤ Korean

----

① Apr 2011 ② Strategies for Utilizing Intellectual Property in Corporate Management ③ Seoul, Korea ④ Korea Forum for Progress, Culture and Creativity - Management Studies Forum ⑤ Korean

----

① April 2011 ② Strategies for Efficient Protection - Maintenance of Intellectual Properties in Korea & Role of IP Lawyers ③ Pohang, Korea ④ Handong University, Law School ⑤ English

----

① Mar - Jun 2011 ② Introduction to Intellectual Property Law, Trademark Act, Design Protection Act, Internet Address Dispute Resolution, Copyright Act ③ Seoul, Korea ④ Korea National Policy University ⑤ Korean

---

① Mar 2011 ② Trademark Act: Law and Practice, Design Protection Act: Law and Practice, Internet Address Dispute Resolution ③ Seoul, Korea ④ Seoul District Bar Association ⑤ Korean

---

① Feb 2011 ② Great Value Arising from Loving the Neighbors ③ Seoul, Korea ④ Ministry of the Interior ⑤ Korean

① Jan 2011 ② Great Value Arising from A Trivial Thought ③ Seoul, Korea ④ The Korea Constitutional Court ⑤ Korean

---

① Nov 2010 ② Strategies for Utilizing Intellectual Property for a Successful Corporate Management ③ Seoul, Korea ④ 61st CEO Breakfast Seminar ⑤ Korean

---

① Oct 2010 ② Trademark Bullies ③ Cheju, Korea ④ APAA 58th Council Meeting ⑤ English

---

① Sep 2010 ② New Marks - Old Law ③ Munich, Germany ④ FICPI 12th Open Forum ⑤ English

---

① Aug 2010 ② Determining Trademark Infringement in Internet Sales - From the Perspective of the Open Market Operator ③ Seoul, Korea ④ Internet and Information Protection Seminar ⑤ Korean

---

① Apr 2010 ② Strategies for Utilizing Intellectual Property for a Successful Corporate Management ③ Seoul, Korea ④ Seo-Il Group for Design Brand Owners ⑤ Korean

---

① Apr 2010 ② Issues in Non-Use Cancellation Actions and Non-Use Trademarks ③ Seoul, Korea ④ 2010 Trademark Forum ⑤ Korean

① Feb 2010 ② Strategies for Utilizing Intellectual Property for a Successful Corporate Management- Comprehensive Intellectual Property ③ Seoul, Korea ④ Fuji Film Korea ⑤ Korean

---

① Jan 2010 ② 最近の韓國デザイン保護法の 主要改正事項および デザイン制度 の主要特徴 ③ Tokyo, Japan ④ Joint Seminar, Korea-Japan Patent Attorneys Association ⑤ Japanese

---

① Dec 2009 ② Trademark Protection of Shapes & Color ③ New Delhi, India ④ FICPI India Symposium ⑤ English

---

① Sep 2009 ② Intellectual Property Society and Strategies for Utilizing Intellectual Property ③ Seoul, Korea ④ Sangam Junior High School - Community University ⑤ Korean

---

① Aug 2009 ② Stories on Brand and Trademark Law - Effective Ways to Protect Brands through Cases Affecting Everyone ③ Seoul, Korea ④ Korean Green Tourism School Graduate Program Workshop ⑤ Korean

---

① Jun 2009 ② Strategies for Utilizing Intellectual Property for a Successful Corporate Management ③ Seoul, Korea ④ NamSeoul Rotary Club ⑤ Korean

---

① Apr 2009 ② Stories on Tradename, Trademarks and Unfair Competition - Introducing Cases on Disputes That Affect Everyone ③ Danyang, Korea ④ Strengthening Competence for Local Government Enforcement Officers ⑤ Korean

---

① Apr 2009 ② Approaches to Using Patent and Trademark Systems ③ Seoul, Korea ④ Korean Industrial Safety Association ⑤ Korean

---

① Nov 2008 ② Characteristics of Korean Design Protection System ③ Pusan, Korea ④ Joint Seminar for Korean-Japanese Patent Attorneys Association ⑤ Korean

---

① Oct 2008 ② Prominent Issues of Korean IP Attorneys' Profession Conflict of Interest, Confidentiality Professional Insurance ③ Seoul, Korea ④ Joint Seminar for Korean-French Patent Attorneys Association (FICPI) ⑤ English

---

① May 2008 ② Similarity in a Global Context ③ Berlin, Germany ④ INTA, 130th Annual Meetings ⑤ English

---

① Mar 2008 ② Border Seizures ③ Seoul, Korea ④ A Korea-Germany Joint Seminar ⑤ English

---

① Mar 2008 ② Strategies for Efficient Protection-Maintenance of Intellectual Properties in Korea ③ Seoul, Korea ④ International Seminar hosted by the U.K. Embassy in Korea ⑤ English

---

① May 2007 ② Understanding the Patent System and Patent Strategies ③ Seoul, Korea ④ Solgo BioMedical Co., Ltd. ⑤ Korean

---

① Mar 2004 ② Effective Trade Mark Rights Enforcement in Asia - Korea, Japan, and China ③ London, U.K. ④ PTMG Annual Meeting ⑤ English

---

① Mar 2005 ② Acquiring Intellectual Property Rights and Maintenance Strategies for Strengthening Company Competitiveness ③ Seoul, Korea ④ Korea Invention Promotion Association ⑤ Korean

---

① Oct 2005 ② Preventing Infringement of Intellectual Property Rights - From the Perspective of Patent Disputes ③ Seoul, Korea ⑤ Korean

---

① Jul 2004 ② Trademark Registration Procedure and Cases on Trademark Disputes ③ Seoul, Korea ④ Korea Agro-Fisheries & Food Trade Corp. ⑤ Korean

---

① Apr 2004 ② Application of Korean Laws relating to Prevention of Cybersquatting ③ Seoul, Korea ④ Domain Name Dispute Resolution Committee ⑤ Korean

① 2004 ② Understanding Patent System and Patent Strategies ③ Seoul, Korea ④ Dong Seoul University ⑤ Korean

---

① Oct 2003 ② Application for Registration of a Brand ③ Seoul, Korea ④ Korea Agro-Fisheries & Food Trade Corp. ⑤ Korean

---

① Sep 2003 ② Trademark Registration Procedure and Ways to File Patents for Agricultural Products ③ Seoul, Korea ④ Continuing Education Program for Agricultural Executives of Kyungki Province ⑤ Korean

---

① May 2003 ② Protection of Bio-related Intellectual Property Rights and Patent Strategies ③ Seoul, Korea ④ 1st Bio-Industries Executive Court, Federation of Korean Industries ⑤ Korean

---

① Mar 2003 ② Transfer of Trademarks in Korea, Licensing, Relief from Damages Sustained in Trading and Strategies for Export Companies ③ Beijing, China ⑤ Korean

---

① 2002 ② The Madrid Protocol and Its Impact on Korean Trademark Laws ③ Seoul, Korea ④ The 3rd Joint Seminar of AIPPI Japan, China and Korea ⑤ English

① 2001 ② Internet Business Model Patents ③ Seoul, Korea ④ The Federation of Korean Industries' e-Business Executive Management Program ⑤ Korean

----

① 2001 ② Protection and Enforcement of Well-Known Trademarks-Service Marks and Domain Names in Korea ③ Tokyo, Japan ④ The Joint Seminar of AIPPI Japan, China, and Korea ⑤ Japanese

----

① Aug 2000 ② Strategies on Patent Disputes and Acquiring Royalties ③ Seoul, Korea ⑤ Korean

----

① Aug 2000 ② Survival Strategies in the Digital Generation - The reason the King of Invention became penniless ③ Seoul, Korea ④ 10th Executive Managers' Book Club ⑤ Korean

■ RESEARCH

Date: 2004

Research Topic: Solutions to Intellectual Property Issues relating to Internet Domain Names

Research Institution: Korea Internet & Security Agency

■ SCHOLARLY PAPERS

① Time / ② Title / ③ Publication / ④ Language Used

----

① 2011 ② Trends in Education of Intellectual Property in Korea ③ "Patent" ④ Japanese

----

① 2012, 2011, 2010, 2009, 2008, 2007, 2006, 2005, 2004, 2003
② The White Paper on Domain Name Disputes (co-author) ③ Korean Internet & Security Agency ④ Korean

----

① May 2007 ② Commentary on STARBUCKS vs. STARPREYA word and device trademarks - in relation to the invalidation actions against [STARPREYA] and [STARPREYA+device] marks ③ Japanese International Intellectual Property Protection Association ④Japanese

---

① 2005 ② Use of Trademark as a Trademark and as a Design ③ Creation and Rights ④ Korean

---

① 2005 ② Revision to the Korean Trademark Act and Design Protection Act ③ AIPPI Japan ④ Japanese

---

① 2005 ② System for Resolution of Domain Name Disputes ③ Korea Internet & Security Agency ④ Korean

---

① Feb 2004 ② The Substantive Standards for Domain Name Dispute Resolution in Korea ③ Book of Scholarly Papers in Celebration of the 60th Birthday of Mr. Myungshin Kim ④ Korean

---

① 2003 ② Protection of Design Registrations for Computer-Generated Graphic Designs in Korea ③ Japanese Economy and Industrial Research Institute, Intellectual Property Information Center ④ Japanese

---

① 2003 ② Korea's Design Application Publication System, Registration System for Certain Products in Designs and Multiple Design Application for Design Registration ③ Journal of AIPPI Japan ④ Japanese

---

① 2002 ② Use of a Mark As a Mark as a Legal Requirement in Respect of Acquisition Maintenance and Infringement of Rights in Korea ③ AIPPI Year Book ④ English

---

① 2002 ② The Madrid Protocol and Its Impact on Korean Trademark Laws ③ Journal of AIPPI Japan Group ④ Japanese

① 2002 ② Trends in Court's Decision on Domain Name Disputes and Legal Reviews on Mediated Decisions ③ KRNIC Joint International Symposium ④ Korean

① 2001 ② Protection and Enforcement of Well-Known Trademarks-Service Marks and Domain Names in Korea ③ Journal of the Japanese Group of AIPPI ④ English

---

① 2000 ② Strategic Use for a Venture Company's BM Patents ③ Venture Capitalist Training Program ④ Korean

---

① 2000 ② Report on decision of similarity of a name mark in connection with an unregistered license as a ground for cancellation of trademark registration under the Trademark Act ③ The Trademark Society ④ Korean

---

① Apr 1998 ② Casebook on Domain Name Disputes ③ National Computer Association ④ Korean

---

1985 Evaluation of and Improving Korea's Policy on Technology Importation (Thesis for the Graduate School of Public Administration, Seoul National University)

■ Your life will be filled with joy when you can shine "your own unique, dazzling light."

"I" am not simply one of 7 billion people. My own unique existence was created in a truly precious time and space. There will never be anything resembling me before and after. I tell my children whenever I can.

"Look at the pebbles on the bank of the river. Each of them looks different. Why are you not as round as me? Why are you triangular? Why are you oblong? Don't complicate things by thinking too much. Take things for what they are. Each of us is different. Because we are all different, there is value in each and every one of us. We follow and benefit from so many things that have been created in the course of mankind, and each one of us has a unique, dazzling formula for life. For this very reason, "I" have a precious and treasured existence. Likewise, we must acknowledge and respect each and every "you" and "them." Each and every one as the world's most unique existence."

You must live with creative best effort. Your life will be filled with joy when you can shine "your own unique, dazzling light." I am certain that your own "light" will contribute to the mankind in its own way.

-From EPILOGUE

DESIGNING YOUR OWN UNIQUE AND DAZZLING LIFE

• FIRST EXPERIENCE IS HEART-POUNDING EXHILARATION

With humility, I wanted to bear witness to how interesting, fulfilling and wonderfully exciting life can be when you live with the belief of the "power of positive force." Regardless of the nature of one's work or education, people strive to achieve their "creative best" output. As a result, one can enjoy the sweet memory of dynamic stories of someone saving a person's life or rescuing a family or even a nation. I can easily imagine how rewarding it would be for a doctor to apply his or her own creative craft to save a person's life despite 1% chance of success.

I am reminded over and over again that the secret to happiness is confronting and overcoming adversities even where creative best efforts did not appear adequate. First experience is heart-pounding electricity. My memories of those first experiences where I took the challenge without cowering are still fresh in my mind. What followed those first experiences energized and excited me as I looked forward to the fruits of my labor.

I also want to share my personal realization of unique and dazzling experiences of "creative best efforts" not only with my peer patent attorneys, but also with all other professionals, business people and my good neighbors on this planet.

-From PROLOGUE-